**DO NOT REMOVE
CARDS FROM POCKET**

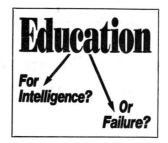

Dr. Bill's 5 Pt. Prescription For What Ails Our Schools

1. Mastery of reading, writing and arithmetic should be a nonnegotiable precondition for promotion to higher grades.

2. Squelch rebellious attitudes that often result in classroom violence and vandalism by requiring youngsters to share responsibility for their education.

3. Abandon the obsolete notion of imprisoning an uninterested child in school until the mandatory age of 16. Insist on mastery of only the basics then leave the rest up to the student and his parents.

4. Put an end to the merry-go-round atmosphere in today's schools where students are shunted from room to room in an endless round of impersonal encounters with specialists who know their subjects, but not their students.

5. Throw out the useless garnish that has been forced on our contemporary schools, but insist on basic, real-world topics that equip kids to cope and function in a complex world.

To David, Elizabeth, and Matthew

With the hope that their
school lives will be enhanced

ACROPOLIS BOOKS
Colortone Building, 2400 17th St., N.W.
Washington, D. C. 20009

Printed in the United States of America by
COLORTONE PRESS, Creative Graphics Inc.
Washington, D. C. 20009

Library of Congress Cataloging in Publication Data

Bills, Robert E.
    Education for intelligence.

    Bibliography: p.
    Includes index.
        1. Public schools—United States.   2. Basic education
—United States.   I. Title
LA217.B54   370'.973   81-19135
ISBN 0-87491-430-2   AACR2

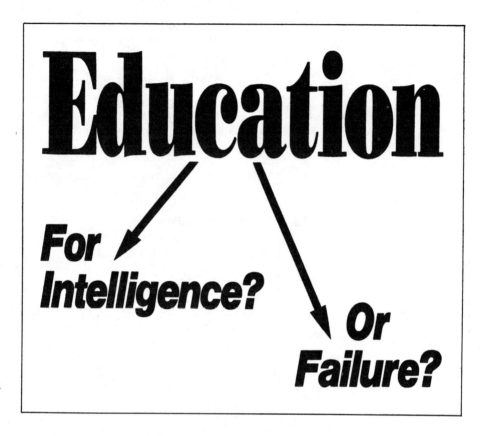

Education

For Intelligence?

Or Failure?

Robert E. Bills, Ed.D.

ACROPOLIS BOOKS LTD.
Washington, D.C.

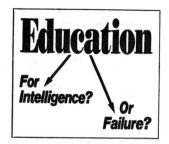

Education

For
Intelligence?

Or
Failure?

Dr. Bill's 5 Pt. Prescription For What Ails Our Schools

1. Mastery of reading, writing and arithmetic should be a nonnegotiable precondition for promotion to higher grades.

2. Squelch rebellious attitudes that often result in classroom violence and vandalism by requiring youngsters to share responsibility for their education.

3. Abandon the obsolete notion of imprisoning an uninterested child in school until the mandatory age of 16. Insist on mastery of only the basics then leave the rest up to the student and his parents.

4. Put an end to the merry-go-round atmosphere in today's schools where students are shunted from room to room in an endless round of impersonal encounters with specialists who know their subjects, but not their students.

5. Throw out the useless garnish that has been forced on our contemporary schools, but insist on basic, real-world topics that equip kids to cope and function in a complex world.

Contents

Preface

The quality of public education is being questioned by many people. Judging by the number of concerned people and the length of time they have been criticizing the schools, there is a problem. But what is it and what can be done about it? A primary purpose of this book is to share my experience gleaned from more than 40 years of study, teaching, administration, and research and the research of some of my students in an effort to answer these and similar questions.

This purpose has had a direct effect on the book. I have attempted to focus broadly on the problems of public elementary and secondary education and their improvement as seen through the lens of my experience and research and the research of my students. Because of this approach, I have not attempted to exhaust the reservoir of research available from other sources. Nor have I attempted to support my views by citing the work of other authors. Instead, the book is the effort of one person, assisted by many, to make sense out of a large and complicated system of interpersonal relationships called public education. It is my hope that the meanings I have discovered in my research and other learnings will be communicated through this book, and that these will stimulate your thinking.

Some Personal Beliefs

My experience has led me to a number of beliefs about the rights of students and the nature of the schools young people need. Many of these can be inferred from this book. Let me make some of them explicit.

I believe that all people — adults and children — have a right to determine their own destinies. Education should serve to make them more effective in doing this.

Second, I believe that every young person has a right to be treated like an important and worthy human being. If we want people to develop intellectually, we must work with them in a warm, human fashion. This is their right and it is their need.

Third, every youngster should have many opportunities for close interaction with warm and responsive teachers. It is only in such a climate of relationships that human potential can develop to its maximum. This means that we must organize schools to permit this to happen. The best method we have discovered for doing this is the self-contained classroom taught by warm, well prepared, and dedicated teachers. Teachers are most effective when they have close interactions with their students over extended periods of time.

Fourth, the flexibility of school programs must be inc eased so they can satisfy the diverse needs of the students affected by them. Flexibility is needed to assure students' intellectual and personal development. Schools should be designed for learners; they should not have to change to fit the schools.

Fifth, people have a right to an education which will help them become competent to maintain themselves. The primary thing we must help them attain through schooling is competence in the fundamental processes so they can function at least minimally in the world in which they will live.

Sixth, all people have a right to as much education as they can profit from and to the type of education which maximally aids their development. This education should be freely available. But no youngster should be forced to accept education beyond the level of competence in the fundamental processes. The price is too high both for the person and for society.

In Appreciation

I am deeply indebted to many people for their help. In particular, I am indebted to the *many* thousands of students who have provided research data. The willingness of public school teachers and administrators to cooperate in efforts to improve schools is gratifying. Without their help, I could not have collected the data shared in this book. Their desire to improve educational opportunities for students is the greatest asset the schools have.

I am indebted to my many students. They have been a source of much personal and intellectual growth. They have encouraged me and have been the source of many excellent ideas.

Doris R. Brown edited this book and has been very helpful. She read the original manuscript and gave many excellent suggestions for its revision and improvement. Her efforts are deeply appreciated.

My friend Jack Frymier was a source of help. He read the manuscript and during the re-writing gave me excellent suggestions for its improvement.

I am especially indebted to my wife, Annie, for her encouragement and forbearance in my work which frequently has consumed too much of my time and energy. Her patience and love have helped me understand more about how we should try to relate to other people. My daughters, Mary Ann and Cathy, also deserve my thanks. I have learned more from watching them grow and develop than I have learned from any other people.

I gratefully acknowledge the willingness of the following publishers to permit me to quote from their publications:

CAPS, Capsule of the University of Michigan for permission to quote from E. J. Shoben, Jr.'s "The New Student: Implications for Personnel Work" which appeared in Volume 2, Number 1 of that publication;

Houghton Mifflin for permission to quote from Carl R. Rogers: *On Becoming a Person.* Copyright © 1961, Houghton

Mifflin Company and from Carl R. Rogers: *Client-Centered Therapy.* Copyright © 1951, renewed 1979, Houghton Mifflin Company;

Alfred A. Knopf, Inc. for permission to quote from *The Prophet* by Kahlil Gibran. The quotation appears on page 56 of that publication and is used by the permission of the copyright holder, Alfred A. Knopf, Inc.

REB
Fall, 1981

Introduction

Why Today's Education is Obsolete

The public believes that students are not learning as they should. They think that teachers are poorly prepared, intellectually deficient, and sometimes derelict in their professional behavior. They believe the schools are in an intellectual crisis.

Since the education of young people is a concern of so many people, many suggestions have been made for its improvement. As might be expected, many are simplistic. They are the kinds of solutions people give when they do not understand problems.

The improvement of education is further complicated by the fictitious beliefs people hold about what education is like and what it can and should do for students. Such beliefs include notions that teachers and other school personnel know what they should do to improve education but they will not do it. Other beliefs relate to what it takes to be an effective teacher and to what people need to become educated. Fictitious beliefs lead to unwarranted criticisms of the schools and to impractical and unproductive suggestions for their improvement.

One of the more frequently heard suggestions for the improvement of education is that schools should be "like they used to be." It is believed that schools once did things which were effective and that since they have quit doing them, they have become ineffective. This suggestion that the educational clock should be turned back to some supposedly more successful period in the history of schools fails to consider the rapidly changing social, political, and economic characteristics of the world in which we presently live. Education, if it is to be effective, must be changed so that it is relevant to this world.

The changing world in which we live affects young people in many ways, and changes in education must be responsive to them. Recent research data show that the longer students remain in school, the more negatively they feel about themselves, about other people, and about their schools. These changes are paralleled by changes in their parents' attitudes toward the schools. The longer students remain in school, the more negatively their parents feel about the schools. Worse still, the longer students remain in school, the more they reject values such as honesty, trustworthiness, reliability, truthfulness, sincerity, cooperativeness, and others of equal importance for them and society.

The blame for these negative changes cannot and should not be placed only on the schools. The profound changes which have occurred and which are occurring in our world have probably had more negative effects on students' development than the schools have had. Our society has sought in many ways to exploit young people to solve its problems.

Within this context of criticism and change, schools have sought to modify and improve their programs and their instructional methods. Many of these attempts to resolve the problems may have exacerbated them. What is needed is a new vision of what schools can do for young people. Suggestions about what schools should become have precipitated serious debate between strong and vocal forces, each contending for its own point of view.

In part, the debate concerns the proper roles of teachers. What constitutes good teaching, and how do good teachers behave in their classrooms? Those who desire a return to earlier educational practices to solve the achievement problem support one type of teacher behavior. Others believe that today's problems can be solved only by new educational practices, so they advocate other types of teacher behavior.

The argument over what is wrong with the schools centers around the question, "What goals should schools help students reach?" One side in the debate believes that education has failed because it has not helped students become well enough informed. Those who believe this also believe that the problem can be resolved by selecting more intelligent and better informed prospective teachers; by requiring that they learn more of what it is appropriate for teachers to know; and by improving their teaching techniques. These people believe that since the teaching of information is the principal job of teachers, the effectiveness of teachers can be measured by tests of their knowledge.

People on the other side of the debate also believe that prospective teachers should be more carefully screened, be more adequately prepared, and use more effective teacher methods. They agree that students should be well informed and should have adequate preparation in basic skills such as reading, writing, and arithmetic. But they also believe this is insufficient. They believe schools exist to create intelligence.

According to this viewpoint, intelligent people are well informed but information alone is insufficient to enable them to behave intelligently. Intelligent behavior also requires adequate self-concepts and concepts of other people, positive attitudes toward self and other people; plus an outlook on life which helps people to recognize problems, bring past experience to bear on their solutions, search for new information and new solutions when past ones prove inadequate, and be open to new experience. According to this view, teaching effectiveness cannot be measured through tests of knowledge. Effective teachers, though knowledgeable, are also able to effect adequate human relationships with their students. Within such relationships, students can become well informed, sensitive, concerned, and open people who are capable of behaving intelligently.

The history of education in this country shows that education has been a constantly changing process. One of its more outstanding features has been its relevance to the times and to the needs of people who supported it. The schools we need today must be responsive to the needs of today's students. With limited and inexpensive changes, education can resolve its problems and become *Education for Intelligence.*

This is what this book is about.

Part I

How We Got Where We Are Today

Chapter One

Popular Beliefs About Education:
True or False?

Many of our beliefs about teaching and learning are mythical. Such beliefs are commonly held but little or no evidence exists to support them. Nevertheless, people cling to such beliefs and defend them.

When change occurs in education, people who believe the myths are convinced that its good has been destroyed. They demand a return to the type and quality of education that they think existed before the "progressive educators" took charge. Their cherished beliefs cause them to view any change as bad and anything new as inferior. One result is that educational progress comes slowly and painfully. Perhaps even more harmful is the tendency to root education in past practices, preparing students for a world which no longer exists. Another consequence is that energy is used in arguing about change instead of evaluating its effects. The most unfortunate result is weakened support for public education. Why spend tax dollars on education when all educators do is waste it on "progressive" experiments? If we are going to improve education, our myths must be examined and seen for what they are.

Fictions such as educational myths are always vague. They appear specific but they are impossible to separate completely. The myths described below demonstrate this characteristic.

Educational Practices Are Valid —

The greatest myth about education is that its procedures, current or past, have been tested. People believe that what is done in classrooms is done because it is known to produce results. They believe that teachers know what children need to learn and how to teach it. There is even less doubt in people's minds that they know what effective teaching is and that it can be measured. None of these beliefs is supported by evidence. Yet the ideas stubbornly persist, affecting the structure of education and the practices of teaching.

Actually, little is known about what constitutes effective teaching. Scientific investigations in this area over the past 75 years or more have added little to our knowledge, in spite of the belief that "everybody knows" what good teaching is and what should be taught.

Teachers Are Not Teaching —

"Since teachers aren't teaching, young people aren't learning." People who hold this popular current belief cling to it even when large-scale achievement tests present contrary evidence. They rationalize that the tests are not as difficult as they used to be, or they point to the fact that half of the students are below average in achievement.

Another part of this myth is that people think they can find out if teachers are teaching by measuring students' achievement. This assumes that achievement tests measure the things that should be learned. It also assumes that schools are completely responsible for what youngsters do or do not learn. And it assumes that all learners are equally capable of learning what is taught and equally desirous of learning it.

A variation of this myth is that children are passive receptacles into which teachers can insert learning. This is the "sausage stuffing" theory of education. It holds that the teacher is the only variable in the learning equation. The teacher teaches, the students learn. Little or no effort is required of students. If they do not learn, the fault is the teacher's.

Effective Teaching Is the Difference —

Following closely is the conviction that if teachers were really teaching, all students would be at or above grade level as measured by achievement tests. This is a version of the myth that good teaching makes all children alike. How many times have we heard, "When I was in school, teachers made you learn!" People who say this usually had little difficulty learning in school and did not notice or do not remember those who did have problems. They may have forgotten that learning was not so easy for themselves either.

Such people also think that the cross section of the school-age population now in school is the same as it was when they were there. This, of course, is not true. Never before has such a large percentage of young people been in school as there is today in this country. This large group includes youngsters who believe learning is important and those who believe school is a waste of time. It includes those who have been read to by loving adults and those who have never been read to. It includes students whose parents play games with them, talk to them, maintain close relationships with them, read for their own information and pleasure, and value education. The group also contains children whose parents do not play with them, do not engage in school-like activities, do not talk to them, and do little or no personal reading. Many of these students question the value of schooling.

In some families, parents are interested in their children's homework and school progress, and help them as much as they can. But a large proportion of parents have no idea of how much homework their children are assigned or how much time they spend on it. The percentage of families in which both parents work outside their homes is increasing rapidly. Time for supervising their children and helping them with their homework is decreasing.

Some students come to school better able to learn than others. They are well rested, well nourished, and healthy.

Others (even from "good" homes) come to school tired, poorly fed, ill, or suffering from chronic conditions which make it difficult for them to learn. All of these different kinds of students can end up in the same classrooms to be taught the same things.

It is commonly believed that a teacher's job is to teach and this is done by telling people what they need to know. The teacher's job is to communicate knowledge to learners. It follows, therefore, that teachers must be well informed, and that they are effective to the degree that they are well informed. But is being well informed enough? All of us have known well informed teachers who taught badly.

Some Students Are Easier to Teach —

My first teaching assignment was in an area described by the United States Department of the Interior as "the greatest non-industrial, non-agricultural, super-rural area in the country." The average yield of corn — the most frequent farm crop — was about 13 bushels per acre (compared to current yields of more than 150 bushels). Youngsters walked as many as seven miles down creek beds to one of the two county highways and were bussed as much as 30 miles each way to school. To do their chores and to be on time for school, many of these young people arose long before daybreak. They often returned, long after sundown, to homes with one or two rooms, no place to study, and no light to study by.

With handicaps like that, it is a wonder that they learned anything. Some of them did not. Some came to school to be with their friends, to spend a winter's day in a warm place, and to avoid the work they would have had to do at home. But there were some who learned. Some graduated, went to college, and became successful professional and business people. On the average, though, achievement test scores showed that the students were not learning as rapidly as students in average schools. So the myths would say that my colleagues and I were poor teachers.

After World War II, I moved to another school. This one drew its students from two diverse groups, working middle-class and economically upper-class. Many of the middle-class students were interested in learning. You told them what they were supposed to learn and they did. Even more of the upper-class students learned rapidly and well. There were few who were not interested in school or learning. Given our achievement test results and the number of graduates who successfully went on to college, my teaching had improved — at least the myths said so.

In my last year of public school teaching, the students were the children of wealth and position. There was only one student who had a serious learning problem in the entire school. It was a pleasure to "teach" this spirited, attractive, and creative group of young people. Almost without exception the graduates of this school went to college and were successful in their chosen work. I must have reached the zenith of my teaching ability.

In the first of these schools, most of the learners were below average. In the second, most were above average. In the third, most were very high achievers. All three schools had good faculties. There were reasons other than teaching effectiveness that caused the differences in the learners' achievement. How much did the teachers in these three schools teach? There was and is no way to know how to answer this question. How much do teachers ever teach? How much is it possible for teachers to teach? The truth probably lies somewhere between the myths that "students learn what teachers teach" and "students are not learning because teachers are not teaching."

Teachers Should Motivate Students —

It is only an assumption that schools ever teach anybody anything. What schools do is offer opportunity and assistance to young people who for the most part bring their motivation to learn to school with them. Teachers sometimes can motivate them to learn, but most of the motivation comes to school with the learners. Their motivation is a product of their families and the quality of their experiences in their preschool years in their homes and communities.

Can teachers make students learn? Probably not. It is much like making a plant grow. You can provide an environment in which the plant can grow but only its internal characteristics can cause it to grow and mature into a plant. Attempts to make the plant grow usually have effects opposite to those desired.

It is deeply ingrained in our society, though, that we can make youngsters grow and develop in desirable directions. An annual State of the Judiciary message by Chief Justice Warren Burger provides an excellent example. He said, "[T]oday we are approaching the status of an impotent society whose capability of maintaining elementary security on the streets, in schools, and in the homes of our people is in doubt." He blamed the schools for at least part of the crime problem because they have "virtually eliminated . . . any effort to teach values of integrity, truth, personal accountability, respect for other's rights [1]."* The results of experimental projects designed to teach moral and ethical values lead us to believe that such values probably cannot be "taught" in school, and probably never were. In spite of the evidence we continue to believe we can make students learn anything if teaching is adequate.

The teachers in one-room rural schools by necessity limited themselves to making assignments and hearing lessons, expecting learning to occur somewhere in between. Most of their students, though sometimes resentful of schoolroom restraints, were there because their parents and even they realized the importance of learning what was being taught. It is different today. Many parents are unable to assist their children's learning. Some do not care if their children learn, and some believe that school is a waste of time. Compulsory laws, however, see that all young people, able or not, interested or not, attend school until about age 16.

All of these factors affect students' learning as measured by standardized achievement tests. Achievement is the product of more than teaching effectiveness.

Grade Placement Can Be Measured —

Almost every human characteristic occurs in a normal distribution. This means that a graph of the characteristic is a bell-shaped curve with most of the people grouped in the middle and only a few at the low and high ends. For example, if the

---

*Throughout the book, numbers included in [ ] refer to references and notes at the end of each chapter.

heights of enough eight-year-old children are measured, the greatest number will be found to cluster around the average height. Some are very short and a few are very tall. About half of the children are shorter than the average eight-year-old and about half are taller. People do not have much trouble understanding the distribution of heights and they are not surprised that half of eight-year-olds are below average in height. Few of them understand the analogy when it comes to the measurement of school achievement — half of all eight-year-olds are below average in achievement.

Even professional educators sometimes fail to understand the meaning of averages. A communication from a state department of education reads, "A major problem of many schools is the fact that almost half of the school student population is reading below grade placement [2]." Grade placement is determined by averaging the scores of a test given to a representative sample of students in a particular grade throughout the country. Thus by definition, half of the children are always below grade placement in the measured ability, just as half of them are always below average in height.

Suppose we measure the reading ability of all students who are in school. Then suppose we discover a new method of teaching reading and all students become far better readers. If we again give our achievement tests, we will find the average score higher than before but half of the scores will still be below average. This is interpreted to mean that half of the students are still below grade placement even though all of the students improved. Achievement tests are re-written and re-averaged (re-normed) about every ten years, and the same thing happens. Regardless of whether all of the children know more about a subject or all of them know less, half will be above grade placement and half will be below. As long as grade placement is used as the standard, half of the children will be doomed to be below grade placement regardless of how well all of the children are reading.

Intelligence, or its measurement as IQ, is computed the same way. The scores of a representative sample of eight-year-olds are obtained and the average is arbitrarily set at 100. Again, half of the children are below average and half are above.

Facetiously, we can say that there is little wonder that half of the children are below average in reading ability since half of them are also below average in intelligence! Half are below average in intelligence for the same reason that half are below average height. When such a system of measurement is used, it is impossible for all of the children to achieve at or above grade placement.

People are confused about grade placement because they believe absolute standards for school achievement exist. They think all pupils in a fifth grade class, for example, should be able to read at the fifth grade level. If the pupils cannot, then it is believed that something is wrong with the teaching. Fifth grade teachers know how well the average fifth grade student can read. They know some will read better than average and some will be below average. They also know the average is different from school to school and from class to class within a school.

It is possible for measured reading abilities in a fifth grade class to range from 1.8 (the lowest score on some grade 5 reading tests) to as high as grade 11. It is, of course, also possible for most or even all the children in a specific class to read above or below grade level for many reasons, some of them unrelated to school. Textbooks are written for students with average achievement in a particular grade. No absolute standard for judging the achievement of learners exists nor has a feasible one ever been suggested.

Good Teaching Decreases Differences —

People assume that the gap in achievement between higher and lower achievers in a classroom can be decreased by more effective teaching. But better teaching widens the gap, not narrows it. Some young people are poorly motivated to attend school and to learn; some receive no help with their schoolwork at home; and some learn slowly no matter what the caliber of teaching. Most youngsters enter first grade reading at 0.0 grade level. By the end of the first year, some will have made more progress than others. Usually, as they continue in school, the same students will continue to make the most progress. So the higher the grade level the greater will be the differences among learners. Teaching that is equally effective for both slow and fast learners helps the slow ones improve but never as much as the fast ones, and the difference becomes more extreme as children advance through school.

Teaching Is Communication —

It is widely assumed that teaching is an act in which a well informed teacher tells less well informed students what they need to know. It is further assumed that the only important thing which happens in a classroom is the learning of information, and that information alone is a sufficient basis for intelligent behavior. People who believe this believe that if people are better informed, their behavior will be more intelligent. This is not true. All of us know well informed people who have little "common" sense. Information plays a part in intelligent behavior, but it is not the only factor.

This set of beliefs has been around a long time. It is so deeply ingrained that anyone who questions it appears foolish. Who questions what philosopher John Locke said when he wrote, "The improvement of ... understanding is for two ends; first, our own increase of knowledge; secondly, to enable us to deliver that knowledge to others." We do not have to go back to Locke to find similar statements of belief. A textbook used in speech courses on many college campuses a few years ago required of prospective teachers contained the following in its preface, "In the classroom to teach is to talk and to learn is to listen." Most scales which purport to measure effective college teaching ask respondents to indicate how well informed the instructor is and how capable in transmitting information. The emphasis on items dealing with information and its transmission in such rating scales shows the importance given these factors in effective teaching by their constructors.

One of my students, James Finch, studied college instructors' effectiveness as judged by their students [3]. His results have been interpreted to say that students base their ratings of instructors' effectiveness more on the instructors' personal qualities than on their teaching behavior. Instructors were judged more by how the students thought the instructors perceived them as people than on the instructors' knowledge, their ability to communicate it, or their teaching styles.

The same point can be illustrated from my personal experience. For many years I have asked students to rate my effectiveness at the end of a term. The scales I use include items on the relationships existing between the students and me as perceived by them. Also included are items that often have no relevance for the course as it was taught. For example, I ask about the effectiveness of my lecturing voice. It so happens that in many small seminar and graduate classes, I do not lecture. Students never hesitate to complete the items. If on the items describing our relationship I receive positive ratings, my voice is rated as effective for my lectures. If, though, the relationship items show that we had a less desirable relationship, my lecturing voice is seen as less effective. The same thing can be said about other items which are irrelevant for some of my courses such as the adequacy of bibliographies, preparation for lectures, and so forth. What the students are rating is not my ability to communicate but the quality of my relationships with them.

Implied in the myth that teaching is merely communication is the belief that effective teachers teach alike. Some teacher education programs support this belief by showing teachers-in-training what to do step by step. The belief is also reflected in college instructor rating scales which use far too few items to describe the many variations in teaching styles, roles, and content which exist. In reality, numerous roles are required for effective teaching. Adequacy of communication is only one of these.

All People Need the Same Education —

Then there is the myth that all people need the same kind of basic education. It is assumed that a basic education stresses reading, writing, and arithmetic. A problem here is the use of the term "basic." If something is basic, then it is obvious that all learners need it. But what is basic and how much of each do students need? Do all of them need the same amount? These questions are not answered satisfactorily by stating that "All young people need as much of the basics as they can learn."

It is frequently assumed that all parents want the same education for their children. In actuality, parents' attitudes vary widely. Some do not care what happens to their children. Others believe teachers know best. Some parents want their children to be prepared for a life better than they had. Other parents have more specific ideas about what constitutes a satisfactory education — that it should emphasize the classics, or prepare for college, or emphasize science and mathematics, and so on.

I once listened to a well-known critic of public education describe the benefits of an education which emphasizes the basics. Such an education would cover not only reading, writing, and arithmetic but history in large doses (he was a history professor), plenty of English language and literature, foreign and ancient languages, art and music appreciation, and massive quantities of science and mathematics. I asked, "What specific subjects would you include in a four-year high school curriculum?" He began to enumerate but it was soon obvious that he realized his effort was futile. The situation reminded me of a PTA I know whose members believed they could strengthen the curriculum of their school, so they designed a one-year study. At the end of the year they were astonished that the faculty found time to cover as many subjects as it did and to cover them so well.

Myths Deter Progress —

The importance of these and other educational myths lies in their unfortunate influence on the public's willingness to support schools and to provide resources for their improvement. When people believe that schools are failing, they withdraw their support. Critical attacks cause teachers and other education professionals who disagree with each other to close ranks, stop discussions of their differences, and kill all hopes of progress. In education as in every aspect of life, the greatest deterrent to progress is the conviction that one's own beliefs are true. If something is true, why question it? If you believe something is true, you will resist efforts to change your opinion.

References

1. *The Miami Herald.* Vol. 71, No. 71, p 1, February 9, 1981.
2. Henderson, D. C. Improved reading programs at the high school level. *The Counselorgram* (Alabama State Department of Education). Volume IV, Number 7, June 29, 1964, p 1.
3. Finch, J. D. *Instructor Openness and Student Evaluation of Teaching Effectiveness.* Unpublished doctoral dissertation. The University of Alabama, 1973.

Chapter Two

Development of American Education:

From Latin Grammar Schools of 1635 to Today's Open Schools

It is commonly believed that schools were more successful in the past than they are now. This belief has led many people to suggest that we should return to earlier practices to improve the schools. Even if it could be accomplished, this would not solve the problems of the schools. American education has been a continuously evolving process, sensitive to the needs and conditions of people and the times.

Change has been the most consistent characteristic of American education. Schools came into existence to satisfy needs; and as needs have changed, so have the schools. Recently the schools have undergone changes in programs, methods, and structure. If these changes have not solved the problems for which they were designed, the solution lies in further modification, not in a return to the past.

Latin Grammar Schools —

Public education in this country dates from a school founded in Boston in 1635 which later became known as the Public Latin

School of Boston. This school was the first of many Latin grammar schools established in the Northeast. Its model came from England where in 1600 there were at least 300 such schools. The English schools taught Latin and Greek for entrance into Oxford or Cambridge, and their American imitators copied their curriculum as preparation to enter Harvard. Greek was taught as a "cultural" subject, but Latin was necessary for preprofessional preparation in the ministry, medicine, or law. Latin grammar schools were not really grammar schools as that term is understood today. Students entered them when they were 8 years old and finished at 15.

Students who completed the seven-year curriculum of the Latin grammar school were proficient in Latin. They had spent much time studying it. Their knowledge of other subjects, though, came through the classics they read. History, natural science, and mathematics were not studied as such. They learned to read English before entering Latin grammar schools, either at home or in schools which existed for this purpose. Arithmetic was added to the course of study in 1814, and in 1819, algebra and geometry were added. These courses were for the preparation of surveyors and navigators. Thus, the purpose of these schools was practical, either vocational or pre-professional preparation.

Early Tax Supported Schools —

In 1642, the Massachusetts Bay Colony General Court directed the selectmen of the town to see that parents and masters taught the children in their care to read English. Nothing was said about schools, but in 1647 the same court ordered the towns to supply teachers to be paid by the inhabitants in general. Thus tax-supported education in this country dates from 1647.

The reason for establishing tax-supported education is interesting in itself. The preamble to what became known as the "Old Deluder Satan Act," which became law on November 11, 1647, stated:

It being one chief project of the old deluder, Satan, to keep men from the knowledge of the Scriptures, as in former times by keeping them in an

unknown tongue, so in these latter times by persuading them from the use
of tongues so that at least the true sense of the original might be clouded
by false glosses of saint-seeming deceivers, that learning might not be
buried in the graves of our fathers in the church and commonwealth, the
Lord assisting our endeavors, it is therefore ordered . . . .

Apparently, the members of the court did not revere Latin and Greek as we are sometimes led to believe. Two reasons were given for compelling the public to support schools — reading scripture and preserving learning. A third reason can be gleaned from other acts of the General Court — publicly supported schools should prepare students to enter Harvard College, which was itself a publicly supported institution at the time.

Schooling and "Culture" —

Education served practical purposes in these early schools. These purposes included ability to read scripture and to avoid the hands of Satan, the preservation of learning, and entrance into college and the professions. Little time was given to "cultural" objectives although to a degree the teaching of Greek was for this purpose. The study of Greek was for "polite" learning.

The trend to preserve culture through schools arose from a desire to continue school practices which no longer had practical value but which had taken on different values. Our best example of this is the study of Latin. Originally, Latin was taught for entrance into professions in which it was necessary — law, medicine, and the ministry. By the end of the 19th century, students' need for Latin had declined and support for Latin as a required course began to crumble.

Eventually the proponents of Latin changed their argument for its support to more general ones — students need Latin to understand English. They pointed to the quality of students who had studied Latin and their superior command of English. Without doubt these were excellent students who would have had good command of English even if they had not studied Latin. Perhaps they would have had a better command of

English if they had applied the time they spent in the study of Latin to the study of English.

Although Professor E. L. Thorndike showed about 75 years ago that the study of Latin does not aid the learning or use of any other language, many people still cherish the belief that it does. The value of Latin in understanding English is argued today even though we know that English is only partially derived from Latin and that English follows its own rules.

When the proponents of Latin sensed that their argument was losing support, they argued that Latin should be taught for its value in "mental" discipline. Still later is was argued that Latin should be taught for its "cultural" value. Practicality was abandoned.

The Academies —

In 1749, Benjamin Franklin proposed that an academy be formed in Philadelphia to offer instruction in English, modern languages, the classics, history, gardening, and good breeding (proper behavior). Some of these subjects were to be taught on an elective basis while others were to be required. Latin and Greek were not on the required list but, probably as a concession to critics, "None that have an ardent desire to learn them should be refused; their English, arithmetic, and other studies absolutely necessary, being at the same time not neglected." Again, the practical need-relevant value of an education was stressed. Franklin's academy opened in Philadelphia in 1751.

Once established, Franklin's academy underwent rapid change and so did not serve as the prototype for the academies which appeared about 25 years later. Four years after its establishment and with a new charter, the name was changed from The Academy and Charitable School in the Province of Pennsylvania to the College and Academy of Philadelphia. The academy included an English school and a school of practical mathematics. The college provided schools of philosophy, Latin, and Greek. Thus the precollege program was need-related and practical; the college part became traditional.

Academies replaced the Latin grammar schools. They had their beginnings in the Phillips Academy of Andover, Massachusetts, which was founded in 1778. Even more than Franklin, its founder, Samuel Phillips, Jr., copied his ideas from the academies of England which had been founded for practical or need-relevant purposes. Unlike the schools established under the Massachusetts law of 1647, this school, and a similar academy founded by Phillips' Uncle John at Exeter, New Hampshire, were not intended to serve as college preparatory institutions. Unlike Franklin's Academy, they never became colleges.

The academies spread along the eastern seaboard and became noted for the breadth and flexibility of their curricula which included most of the then known sciences and arts. *Entrance requirements were minimal and courses of study tailored to the interests of the students.* So in terms of curriculum, these academies differed significantly from Franklin's.

The academies disappeared about 1900 except for isolated ones supported by wealthy families. They were in large part replaced by high schools which probably had their beginnings in the English Classical School opened in 1821 in Boston, which later changed its name to the English High School. A principal reason for the founding of the English Classical School was that the free primary schools of reading and writing did not go far enough in educating students. Thus many parents were forced to send their children away from home to attend academies. The three-year course of study included such subjects as navigation, surveying, moral and political philosophy, algebra, geometry, logic, history, bookkeeping, and natural theology. Again, the practical need relevance of American schools was evident.

Compulsory Education —

During the period of development of the academies and high schools, there were parallel developments in free and common schools throughout the states at what would now be called the elementary level. Free in this sense meant that the schools did not charge tuition; common meant that they emphasized the common branches of learning, namely reading and writing. The curriculum of these common schools included reading, writing, arithmetic, orothography (writing, penmanship, and spelling), and "decent behavior."

In 1789, Massachusetts passed a law "to provide for the instruction of youth, and for the promotion of good education." Common schools were established in Virginia in 1846 when statewide provision was made for free primary schools to be attended on a permissive basis. Other states included in the early movement for free primary schools were New York and Pennsylvania. These schools were established to satisfy practical needs.

One of the last ingredients needed for our modern school system was added in 1852 when Massachusetts passed the first compulsory school attendance law. All children between the ages of 8 and 14 were required to attend school at least 12 weeks each year, if their town or city provided schools for that long a period of time. By 1890, 27 states and territories had enacted compulsory attendance laws. These laws were enacted in part to shelter children from industrial exploitation.

Education and Need-Satisfaction —

A predominant characteristic of American education apparent even in this brief history is change. In almost all instances, this change has been effected by a desire to make education more readily available and more responsive to the needs of students. As need has changed, education has changed. Seldom has the change been reactionary; almost always it has been toward the better satisfaction of the needs of greater numbers of people.

A second important characteristic of the development of American education is that, unlike secondary education, there has never been serious disagreement about what should be accomplished through the primary schools. On the other hand, there has never been strong agreement about the purpose of secondary education; in fact, since the formation of high schools, there has been serious disagreement.

A third characteristic has been the need-relevant character of American education. Primary and secondary schools were never formed to provide "cultural" or general education. The so-called cultural subjects were included originally because of their practical value for educated people, and thus were means to ends and not ends in themselves. Schools were formed in response to the concrete needs of students. "Cultural" subjects were included only in response to demands to protect the status quo.

Separateness of Primary and Secondary Education —

A fourth characteristic of American education has been the separate development of elementary and secondary education and the different needs they serve. Elementary education was formed around the subject matter deemed necessary for maintenance of self-organization. With an elementary school education, people could inform themselves about practical matters such as religion and politics. An elementary school education provided the essentials for being informed and functioning intelligently in society.

Because elementary schools were viewed as ends in themselves, secondary schools did not require prior elementary school attendance, although they did require that students be able to read and to write before admission. High schools and their forerunners were designed to prepare students for college-level work and some specific vocations.

Secondary education was formed around subjects formerly needed for vocations such as surveying or navigation or for further college-level professional preparation. These subjects were meaningful for students, as were the primary school subjects, but their usefulness was for enhancement of existence. Primary school subjects were needed for living; secondary school subjects were needed for vocational and preprofessional preparation.

The distinction is an important one. Historically, secondary schools have existed to prepare students for college while elementary schools have been ends in themselves. Today, though, we have come to view elementary education as preparation for high school entrance. Quite likely this is because all children attend elementary school, and most continue on to high school. The continuity which supposedly exists between elementary and secondary education has been imposed on elementary schools; it is not an outgrowth of their functions. Students should be ready for high school work when they complete elementary school. But the goal of an elementary education is seriously distorted when it is seen as preparation for high school. The goal is survival and intelligent functioning in society.

The needs of students which are satisfied through elementary education are different from those of secondary education. Apparently this distinction is not understood. Many people seem to have concluded that since elementary education is meaningful for students, secondary education which begins where elementary education ends is also meaningful. Such an assumption is unwarranted. The majority of today's high school students find the curriculum irrelevant. This irrelevancy is basic to many of the problems presented by high school students and many of the findings reported in this book.

What makes the argument important is that the more we see elementary education as preparation for secondary education, the more we make elementary schools resemble secondary schools. The more we see elementary schools like secondary schools, the easier it is to lose sight of the special goals of elementary education.

Perhaps the point can be made clearer by looking at the relationship between high schools and colleges. Because high schools developed as college preparatory institutions, their programs resemble college programs. They look like mini-colleges. To better prepare students for college work, the trend has been to make high schools more like colleges although the majority of the students who enter them will never attend college.

If students need more education for successful living than provided by elementary schools, secondary education must be redesigned for them. Educators have recognized this as a serious problem. The solutions, though, have been inadequate. They have attempted to modify the high school curriculum for students who are not college-bound while keeping its essential college preparatory nature. This does not work. Almost invariably, students in the modified high school programs are seen as having less personal worth than those planning to attend college. Furthermore, the modified, watered-down curriculum does not satisfy the needs of the college-bound either. The solution to the problem of non-college-bound students lies in effecting a separation of the dual schools which secondary schools have become. A meaningful curriculum could then be developed for the large group of high school students who today do not find personal meaning in what they are studying.

This differentiation of elementary and secondary education may seem unimportant until we realize that one of the major forces which has changed the elementary school curriculum in the past few years has been the downward extension of subject-matter instruction, attempting further to make elementary schools preparatory schools for secondary education. This one factor probably accounts more for the disruption of elementary education and elementary school children than any other. The research reported in this book supports the conclusion that elementary school children are troubled. It shows, also, that high school students have even greater problems.

The reason for the downward extension of high school type of instruction was an honest one. It was believed that high school students were not achieving at high enough levels because, it was reasoned, they were not properly prepared. Elementary school programs were modified accordingly, and the artificial continuity between these two different kinds of schools was further cemented. In this way the individuality and integrity of elementary school programs and their special methods of instruction have been damaged. We also have lost sight of the need-relevant and practical purposes of elementary education, subjugating these to high school preparation.

The purpose of secondary education has in large part remained college preparation even though the large majority of students who *enter* high school never plan to attend college and will not attend. Thus, the purpose of elementary education also has become college preparation. When looked at in terms of the needs of elementary school children, this is lamentable. Worse still, the trend has resulted in destroying the unique strengths of elementary schools, forcing their instructional methodologies to resemble those of secondary schools which are even more poorly suited for elementary school children than they are for high school students. High school instructional methods have continued to ape college methods.

Recent Efforts to Improve Education

Most of the changes in elementary schools in the past two decades resulted from questions about the adequacy of American education. These questions were not necessarily valid for elementary schools. The failure of the United States to launch the first earth satellite was due supposedly to inadequacies in our educational programs. The facts, however, do not support such a conclusion. The United States did not elect to enter the "space race" as early as Russia did. As a result Russia launched a satellite before we did. When President Kennedy said that we would put a man on the moon by the end of the 1960s, we proceeded to do so. The blame for falling behind in the space race was placed on the schools instead of on the politicians where it should have been.

National Science Curricula —

One response to the launching of Sputnik was an effort to redesign and strengthen curriculum and instruction in the high schools. The first efforts to improve high school courses was through the National Defense Education Act and by the National Science Foundation. These efforts included attempts to redesign high school science and mathematics courses and improve the teaching of these subjects.

One of these involved the introduction of the "new math." This effort, sponsored by professional mathematicians (although when it went "sour" education was blamed for it), attempted to make arithmetic into mathematics. Its consequence seems to have been a generation of children less literate in solving arithmetic problems than their predecessors. Recent national surveys have shown that students know more about mathematics today than ever before, but they they are less able to apply it to solve important practical problems than students of a few years ago.

Other Federal Efforts —

The efforts of the National Science Foundation to change American education were small in respect to others such as the National Defense Education Act, the Education Professions

Development Act, and the Elementary-Secondary Education Act. The Elementary-Secondary Education Act especially has encouraged experimentation and research in both elementary and secondary education, funneling vast sums of money into the effort. Schools have been encouraged to experiment with new curricula and new instructional methods.

There is little reason to believe that the expenditure of time and money by the United States Government for the improvement of education has been successful. This is probably due to three things. The first is the fact that American educators are not researchers. When they attempt to experiment with curricula and methods, they have to turn to outside experts for advice and assistance. The experts have not always been dedicated to helping schools improve. Nor have they always been prepared to or wanted to help the schools do the things the schools feel they should do.

A second important reason why federal support has not been helpful to schools lies in the "strings" attached to the grants. Seldom have schools been given funds to assist them in doing the things they knew they should be doing. Instead, the funds have been given for innovative procedures and methods, leaving the schools with less time to accomplish their basic tasks.

The third reason for the failure of federal programs has been the assumption about what changes need to be made to improve the schools. It was assumed that the way to improve schools is by improving the amount and quality of subject-matter. Supposedly, if subject-matter learning is improved, students will be better prepared for college level study and will become the technicians and scientists America needs. Proposals for federal projects which have not adopted this assumption have only infrequently received funding. For most students, though, the subject-matter being taught in high schools is still not meaningful. As a result, students are not learning more with the newer methods and content than previous students did.

The schools have assumed that people need what they are being taught. Schools could be improved, therefore, by increasing the amount being learned. One consequence has been that much of the educational research of the past 25 years has been directed toward helping students learn more of the subject-matter which it is assumed that they need. The evidence shows that this goal is not being achieved.

Recent Changes in School Organization

A major consequence of the attempt to teach more subject-matter has been the extension of departmentalized instruction into the elementary school. (This attempt has also furthered the assumption that elementary schools exist to prepare students for high schools.) Departmentalization is the form of organization for instruction used in most colleges and universities. Its purpose is to group together instructors with similar interests so that they will stimulate each other. Furthermore, they can specialize in teaching various aspects of the subject.

Because of the subject-matter orientation of the high school curriculum, large schools also organize instruction around departments. Their belief is that if this organization helps colleges, it should also help high schools. They see little difference in their instructional purposes.

In the small high schools which previously existed, teachers did not group themselves according to specialization. Instead, they grouped themselves as a faculty, their concerns being for the entire school program and its consequences for students. In particular, they were concerned about the development of individual children. As high schools have grown in size and departmentalized, they have become more impersonal. Their concerns have shifted from students to instruction. One reason why small high schools were consolidated into large ones was the belief that the larger schools could provide teachers with greater expertise in their fields. The negative consequences for students are presented throughout this book.

In the 1920s and earlier, most schools in the United States were organized into what is called an 8-4 plan, eight grades in elementary school and four in high school. At that time, elementary school was the limit of education for most children. With increased need for specialization and the depression of the 1930s, more young people began to attend high schools and to think of attending college. In 1930, less than one-third of the children who completed elementary school attended high school. The depression accounted for large increases in high school enrollments. If elementary school graduates could not get a job, they might as well get more education. Even though many people with college degrees were selling shoes, they at least had jobs.

It was believed at that time that one factor which limited high school attendance was the "gap" between self-contained elementary classrooms and the subject-matter centered instruction of high schools. Shifting from one classroom to another was supposedly confusing to students. So, junior high schools were introduced to narrow this gap, and to group together preadolescent children whose interests and level of physical development separated them from students in grades 10-12. The junior high school was proposed as an exploratory school in which children could begin to set goals for their futures. This ideal was never realized. Junior high schools resembled senior high schools in curriculum and instructional methods. Furthermore, the gap which existed between grades 8 and 9 had now been shifted downward to between grades 6 and 7 where children were even more poorly equipped by lack of maturation to cope with it.

Junior high schools are now being replaced by middle schools. In most instances, middle schools include grades 5 through 8. Their purpose is to offer students an exploratory period and to give them a wide range of experience. (What short memories we have!) Some schools seems successful in achieving this purpose, but in many middle schools, instruction is departmentalized and textbook-centered. In most of these schools, children change from one classroom to another for much of their instruction. Departmentalized middle schools closely resemble the junior high schools they replaced; and thus in these schools the gap between elementary and secondary education has been lowered to between grades 4 and 5.

The middle schools formed to give children unique learning experiences also have tried to provide exploratory activities and broaden the scope of children's experience. Many middle schools were formed, however, for less lofty motives such as dealing with shifting community populations, increased enrollments in middle grades, and court-ordered integration. Schools formed for such reasons almost always offer textbook-centered instruction. The more innovative middle schools are motivated by a desire to improve educational opportunities, the less innovative ones to cope with problems. Even in the more innovative middle schools, though, there has been an increase in subject-matter emphasis; the less innovative schools have managed to push the secondary school philosophy down to grade 5 and sometimes lower.

The pressure for subject-matter concentration has not been eased by the advent of middle schools. Some self-appointed reformers have advocated that instruction be given by specialists even in the first grade. Children would be taught reading by reading specialists, arithmetic by arithmetic specialists, and so forth. One thing this assumes is that to teach children what they need to know does not require teachers to know the children as people. It also assumes that the only important factors to consider in adequate instruction are knowledge of subject-matter and teaching techniques. Under such assumptions, it is easy to understand why the research presented in this book reflects so negative a picture.

Elementary School Organization

Barbara Lawhon, one of my students, studied two groups of schools. One set of these schools included only middle schools in each of which students were given departmentalized instruction. The second set of schools were elementary schools in which pupils were taught in self-contained classrooms; only grades 5 through 8 of these elementary schools were studied. Lawhon then compared the type of decision-making and the qualities of teachers' relationships with students in these two different kinds of schools.

As was expected, Lawhon found highly significant differences between the middle schools and the elementary schools. Students in the elementary schools report that they have more opportunities to make decisions for themselves and to interact with their teachers and other students in making decisions than are reported by the middle school students. The middle school teachers were described as more teacher-centered than the elementary school teachers. Relationships with the elementary teachers were somewhat superior to those with the middle school teachers.

Lawhon found that at the fifth grade level, differences in the two types of schools were not significant. This bears out the observation that fifth grade teachers tend to teach like elementary school teachers regardless of the type of school organization, and that differences in teachers' instructional methods become greater with increases in grade level. It is probably also true that middle school teachers attempt to relate to their students in the way they would in self-contained classrooms, since they still see the pupils at this school level as children. However, the greater number of students middle school teachers have each day probably decreases their opportunity to know them as individuals. Hence decision-making and interpersonal relationships suffer.

Open Schools and Self-Contained Classrooms

One characteristic of human nature is that when our efforts are unsuccessful we may conclude that we did not try hard enough. The next time we try harder; we do not question the assumptions on which our efforts are based. It is assumed that schools exist only to teach subject-matter, and the best way to do this is to be textbook-centered. As evidence has accumulated that what schools are doing is not accomplishing what many people desire, we do not reexamine our premises. Instead we conclude that our teachers are not very good.

Since students are not learning substantially more even though schools are using "innovative" methods, educators have concluded that they must "individualize" instruction and sometimes require "mastery" learning on an individualized basis. What is done under these rubrics is anything but individualized. In general the approach is to develop materials which youngsters can study at their own pace with assistance from their teachers. When students feel they have gained command of the topic, they are tested. These tests supposedly assess a student's learning problems, and also determine if the student is ready to move on to the next topic. The student determines the pace of the learning. This type of "individualized" instruction is called *continuous progress instruction*.

In some types of "individualized" instruction, students are given even greater rein in determining their direction and pace. Such instruction appears in many schools under the names of *open instruction, open classrooms,* or *open schools.* Some of these schools use learning centers to individualize their instruction. Others use other techniques. But the object remains the same: to "individualize" instruction.

Although such teaching is called individualized, it really is not. Sometimes the learners are told something like, "Take your own time and set your own pace. We, the teachers, are here to assist you." But there comes a day of reckoning. Students are *all* expected to arrive in the same place at the same time. If they do not, woe unto the stragglers. Neither the content nor the amount to be learned have been individualized. The goals of the learning are the same for all the learners.

Individualized instruction was used in the open-space schools included in a study I conducted which compared four open-space schools with four traditional schools. Each of the schools contained grades K through 6 in a large school system organized on a 6-3-3 plan. Each of the open-space schools was constructed without interior walls. There was a materials center in the middle of the open space and carpeting throughout. Each school used a variety of individualized instructional methods but leaned heavily on continuous progress instruction, two of them exclusively. The elementary schools were traditional and organized into self-contained classrooms.

The open-space schools were matched as nearly as possible with traditional schools within the same school system on the basis of the socio-economic levels of parents, racial mixtures of students, and sizes of the schools. The open-space schools had an average of 998 pupils, the traditional elementary schools 810. Each school had about 25 per cent black children, the majority transported from inner-city school districts. Although the open-space schools were climate-controlled and carpeted throughout, the traditional schools were capable only of being heated. They had no carpets.

Instruction in the traditional schools was excellent as judged by what usually occurs in such settings. And the situation in the open schools was ideal as judged by what most authorities would recommend for such schools. The open-space teachers spent far more time together in planning their work with the children than is done in most schools. They worked in "pods" or small units of four classes clustered together within the open space, permitting maximum flexibility in grouping for instruction.

The results of the study indicate that the open-space schools have both strong and weak points; parents are more favorably inclined toward them and their pupils are better adjusted. However, open-space pupils are not significantly different from traditional school students in their attitudes toward their schools. In addition, the open-space schools are more teacher-dominated than the traditional schools; the relationships of pupils with their teachers are less positive; and teachers interact less with their students in making decisions.

As judged by the academic achievement of the students, the traditional schools are superior to the open-space schools in spite of the fact that the open-space teachers were judged to be better teachers. Furthermore, the evidence indicates that the longer students remain in these open-space schools, the greater their learning deficit becomes. Based on all of these comparisons, it was concluded that the traditional schools are superior to the open-space schools.

The structure of the open-space schools tends to dictate the instructional methodology of the teachers, and thus, these four schools are similar to each other. The traditional schools do not suffer the same restrictions and so are more heterogeneous. The heterogeneity is reflected in the attitudes of pupils toward their schools and in decision-making and interpersonal relationships with teachers. Students in the traditional schools are subject to a wider range of teacher effectiveness than those in the open-space schools. This is sometimes used as a reason for departmentalizing instruction; it shares the less effective teachers with all of the students and not just with one classroom. It is a matter of opinion as to whether it is better for many children to be exposed to such teachers or if a few children should get a more concentrated dose.

If teachers were free to select their own instructional methods and match those with their capabilities and individual characteristics, in the long run better instruction would result. There is no one best way to teach. Teaching is an interpersonal relationship, and teachers must discover how they can become the best tools for the development of boys and girls. *You cannot be me and behave like I do. Even if I were able to use my talents successfully, you could not hope to be successful trying to be like me. You must be yourself because your experience is unique.* Only when people are consistent with the meanings of their own experience can they provide consistent and congruent relationships to aid the development of other people.

Did the open-space teachers have freedom to teach in the best ways they could? The teachers in these open-space schools did not have the privilege of being themselves. The high noise level in the open space schools coupled with a lack of any place in which to conduct discussions with children in groups or to encourage discussions among children (for example, in show-and-tell periods) accounts for many of the negative results. As a consequence of the noise and structure, teachers tended to call their groups together, gave directions, and sent the children off to do their work individually.

The open-space teachers planned together and developed excellent relationships with each other but not with their students. Thus the open-space teachers were seen by their students as teacher-centered and having inadequate relationships with them. Additionally, the high noise levels and inability to control the level of the light severely limited the use and effectiveness of audio-visual materials and sharing opportunities. So the structure of the buildings tended to dictate the instructional patterns. The open-space teachers had less opportunity to discover how they could be effective, and they were less free to teach in ways in which they could be most effective.

Teaching in "innovative" ways does not necessarily yield improved results. Recent efforts to improve schools have caused them to become more impersonal and less need-relevant.

Chapter Three

Fast Changes:
Experiencing
Our Children's World

Many adults seem to believe that our children's world is the same as it has always been. Consequently they want to educate children as they think children were educated when schools were "more successful." This assumes that students' needs are the same as they used to be and that schools were successful at that time. Are their beliefs valid? Even a superficial examination of the world in which we live today shows they are not. This is important. If education is to be effective, it must be relevant to people's needs in the world in which they live.

Our Changing World —

It is comforting to believe that the way things are today is the way they have always been. But life has never been simple; it has always been changing, and today it is changing more rapidly than ever before. One of the more important features of modern living is the speed with which change occurs and the many aspects of our lives affected by it.

In retrospect, life as little as 25 or 30 years ago seems simple.

In 1950, few people had television sets; most wives worked at home; few homes had window air-conditioners and home central air-conditioning was almost unheard of; husbands were the "breadwinners"; only a few homes had appliances such as automatic clothes washers, clothes dryers, and dishwashers; and violence and vandalism were practically nonexistent in middle America. Business was usually conducted on a face-to-face basis with people you knew. Most collecting, billing, ordering, and accounting were hand operations. Important business transactions often were sealed with a handshake.

In contrast, though, what were simple business transactions yesterday are often complicated affairs today. This is due, in part, to impersonal human relationships, mechanical failures and mistakes, greater numbers of people, changes in ways of doing things, greater volumes of business, greater psychological distances among people, and to the complexity of the machines and processes used. Employees usually do not know their customers and often do not care if customers' needs are satisfied. One consequence is that many things are done incorrectly the first time and much effort is wasted in correcting errors.

Today even the simplest machines are far more complicated than those of the 1950s. In 1950, the average man could point to the parts of an automobile under the hood and tell you what they were even though he might not have completely understood their functions and did not always know how to repair them [1]. The average person today has little idea of what the parts are under the hood. Even fewer know how to repair them.

The complexity of life threatens to overwhelm us, and we try to insulate ourselves against it by not becoming involved. Consequently we appear apathetic. We often settle for less than we bargained for because it is too difficult to get what we purchased in perfect working condition or to get the adjustments necessary for remedying its defects. We lack the time to persist in getting what we ordered or in getting an unflawed product. We even lack the understanding necessary to know if the product we receive is in satisfactory working condition. We do not know what to do to get problems rectified.

Frequently we feel that we have lost control of our lives.

This is especially true in health matters. Each day brings new announcements of major health hazards in water, food, air, clothes, toys, and machinery. The list of hazards seems inexhaustible and efforts to avoid them appear futile. Our efforts to avoid difficulties are ineffective, and difficulties encountered in solving problems often lead us to conclude that the solutions are not worth the effort.

The complexity of "modern" living affects young people as well as adults. For example, parents are so busy with things they must do that they have little time for their children. Their children frequently are unsupervised and undisciplined. Children often are permitted unlimited freedom because of the absence of their parents and their control. Youngsters frequently choose their own diets and select their own bedtimes. They learn their moral principles without their parents' assistance. Too often, children are deprived of their parents' guidance and are as confused as their parents.

The Extensiveness of Change —

It is difficult to comprehend the extensiveness of the change which has occurred during the past 25 or 30 years. Color television was not available; rocketry, except for the crude machines used in World War II, was undeveloped; computers were only coming into existence and commercially manufactured machines were not available; federal aid to education was minimal; money was "tight"; and most people "made do" with what they had or did without. Questions about what school curricula should contain and how much children should know appeared easily answerable. Education was to prepare people for life. Even though life was complex, people could still act as if they understood it and know what young people needed for successfully living in it.

Professor E. J. Shoben, Jr. described the situation clearly when he wrote in 1968:

In our generation, it was still possible to believe on good grounds, that the man who mastered yesterday's experience was best prepared to cope with tomorrow's problems. The current rate of social change just doesn't allow easy acceptance of this kind of doctrine. Possibly, the man most in command of yesterday's traditions because he is committed to them, is least equipped to deal with tomorrow's problems. A good deal of the impetus for curricular reform grows out of student conviction that there is no longer any assurance that yesterday's traditions are the best preparation for the problems of tomorrow [2].

Change is inevitable. People accept the status quo only when it is not possible to move beyond it. They seek to enhance themselves and their existences. History can be viewed as the efforts of people to gain greater control over their destinies. When they do this, they seek to change the circumstances of their existences.

The Search for Destiny —

What sets the current age apart from those which preceded it is the accelerated rate of people's efforts to gain control over their destinies and the human conflicts these efforts have generated. The conflicts usually are between people who seek enhancement of opportunity and those who believe their choice will be diminished if the other people prevail. The clamor for greater opportunity and equal status comes in waves.

These tides in the struggles of people are not easily stemmed. Could the people of India have stopped struggling for their independence? Could the many colonial nations which sought independent existences since World War II have been expected to restrain themselves forever? During the past 35 years we have seen the dissolution of colonial empires which had existed for half a millenium. The people who were subjugated in these empires sought greater control over their lives and destinies. It was inevitable that black people in this country would mount their struggle for a greater voice in their destiny. And it is not surprising that women have continued to express their desires for greater autonomy, freedom, and equality.

It is inevitable that changes of the magnitude which have occurred since World War II would affect our young people and their desires to be treated in more humane ways. Their insistence on being recognized as human has caused radical changes in instructional methods, classroom disciplinary

Fast Changes

procedures, and curricular offerings. All too often schools have been frustratingly slow to recognize the need for change and to accept it. They have been even slower to initiate change.

An important characteristic of the period in which we live is the demand of people who feel subjugated for freedom *now*. Often such groups of people compete with each other for freedom, and all of them inevitably find themselves in conflict with groups which currently have power and privileged status. These conflicts have led us as a nation to lack conviction about what is right and fair. How do we deal with change of such magnitude? How do we resolve the many conflicts and satisfy the many reasonable demands? Lacking an answer to the question, we ignore, stall, compromise, and at times appease. But the demands do not disappear. Their proponents lobby and exert other pressures to win advantages for themselves.

The inevitability of change does not make it easier for parents and schools to respond to young people who demand change and freedom and who demand them *now*. A frightening aspect of the need for a changed society is the lack of clarity in the direction in which we should change. Adults fear the destruction of a way of life which, although flawed, may be able to satisfy human need better than that which would replace it.

Change and the Schools —

During the past two to three decades, demands for equality and improved schools have resulted in significant changes in the structure and methods of education. Schools have been used by society as the primary instrument to effect change in itself. Some changes in the schools have resulted from changed relationships among people such as desegregation, equality of women and men students, and increased recognition of civil rights in general. Others are the results of political and economic changes such as the launching of Sputnik and the space age and the increase in the number of wives who work outside their homes.

Some changes in the schools are so extensive that relationships between young people and their teachers have been revolutionized. For example, schools have been defendants in law suits in an unprecedented degree. The results have altered relationships between teachers and their students. Teachers often feel helpless when it comes to controlling students; many of their former means of discipline have been declared illegal and adequate substitutes have not been found. Another changed relationship has been between parents and their children's teachers. Teachers report that they no longer can count on the support of parents in matters of learning and discipline. Many parents act as if teachers were antagonists.

Economic opportunity and assistance programs have also had direct effects on schools and their programs. For example, a wealth of materials and remedial programs is now available to "poor" schools. The number of children who receive assistance through free breakfast and lunch programs and by other means has increased markedly. One consequence has been that black children and the children of the poor in general are in attendance and remain in school for longer periods of time than ever before. A second consequence is that school-age children have had better opportunities to witness cultural differences and be affected by them.

As expected, court-ordered school desegregation has directly affected schools. Children of different races and of different socio-economic levels attend school together in a degree never before known in this country. Efforts to rid schools of race, ethnic, religious, and sex biases have affected curricula, subject-matter content, methods of grouping students, instructional materials, and methods of instruction. Teachers also have been affected by the changes. They are uncertain about what to teach, how to teach, and how to satisfy the many and diverse demands placed on them.

Changes in Child Rearing —

Since the 1940s, there have been marked changes in the ways parents relate to their children. Veterans returning from World War II were weary of conflict, uncertainty, and insecurity. They want to marry, settle down, and have families. They married and the birthrate soared.

The children of these families were so important to their parents that they became avid consumers of a new psychology of child rearing. This psychology emphasized that children have rights and should be permitted to be themselves and have their needs satisfied. But supposedly out of love, sometimes out of neglect, and frequently because of lack of time, many parents in the 1960s and 1970s failed to differentiate between permissiveness and license. The economy was strong, material objects and physical comforts were easy to obtain, and pressures from children were great. Why deny children what they want? If something is broken, do not try to fix it. Do not worry about taking care of things. They can always be replaced. "Throw it away and buy something new" became the creed of many working people. If you cannot pay for it, buy it on credit. The important thing is to have it, regardless of cost, and have it now.

Children reared under these conditions require different instructional relationships than those reared under more restrictive methods. Children who have been given license rebel at autocratic methods and become discipline problems. On the other hand, children reared under more highly controlled methods may become discipline problems in more permissive classrooms. Thus teachers are faced with a dilemma. Their methods may be harsher than some students can accept while being too soft for others.

Two Different Worlds —

It is difficult for adults reared during the depression of the 1930s to realize the differences which separate them from today's children. During the 1930s, most of the efforts of people were bent toward maintaining themselves. Securing life's necessities required long working days and stringent sacrifices. Purchases were limited to absolute essentials. Many people had little idea of where their next meal would come from and worried about finding money for clothes, medical care, heat, and the next month's rent. Clothes for the average person were severely restricted in quantity and conservative in style, and were repaired as long as possible. Entertainment came from things such as listening to radio programs, playing games with family members and friends, visiting relatives, making candy, popping corn, reading, and other simple pleasures.

Many of today's children have never known want or a need

to economize. For them, personal sacrifice is a foreign concept. Instead they have been reared in a world of abundance in which their many desires are interpreted as needs by their parents and quickly satisfied. Maintenance of self has become automatic and expected. The concerns of these children have centered around enhancement — how to have the same things and the same privileges "as everybody else" and more. For many young people, enhancement in a material sense is readily available.

Our young people live in a different world from that of their parents and grandparents. A few years ago this difference was called a "generation gap." Anyone over 30 years of age was considered "irrelevant" because younger people perceived things differently from "old" people over 30. The gulf that separates many parents and teachers from children is wide. Many adults believe they should save for a "rainy day" while their children have never known anything but sunshine. What is an extravagance for a parent may be a bare existence for a child.

One consequence of the philosophy of abundance is that many youngsters do not have a locus of control. They are not controlled by their parents, and they have not learned to control themselves. Because their parents seem to have forgotten the word "no," children often find themselves without external guidance or internal guides for their behavior, and bewildered by the multitude of choices and the lack of guidelines for making choices. Their bewilderment is frequently matched by that of their parents who cannot understand them. They present difficult instructional problems.

The "Now" and "Me" Generations —

The ready availability of material things has led young people to demand instant gratification. They want what they want and they want it *now*. Consequently, the youth of the late 1960s and the early 1970s were characterized as the "Now Generation."

The "Now Generation" yielded quickly to another. The belief that it is only right to have all desires satisfied and have them satisfied *now* gave rise to an "I" or "me" generation. The effects of the "me" generation have been so pervasive that they have even changed the structure of our language. Although it formerly was considered poor taste to name oneself before naming another, many people place themselves first in their thinking. The sentence, "Johnny and I —" changed to "I and Johnny —" or "Me and Johnny." Even mature adults were affected by it. For example, President Carter said, following a rearrangement of his cabinet, "There is absolutely no doubt in my mind that I and my administration...."

The egocentric thinking of the "me" generation poses additional problems for teacher-student relationships. Students do not want to wait their turns and are frequently uncooperative. They resent having to wait in line and resist the discipline necessary for classroom order. Some have such a problem of waiting that they appear hyperactive.

Self-centered children present difficult instructional problems. Instruction not recognized as relevant is rejected as authoritarian and abusive. Motivation to learn, except that which is seen immediately as relevant, is minimal. Such problems are a part of the present educational context.

Sputnik and Exploitation —

Russia's launching of Sputnik, the first artificial earth satellite, and the entrance of our country into the space race had profound effects on education. Massive federal aid to the schools was stimulated by what was perceived as a failure of the schools to produce technical proficiency in mathematics and science. The first federal efforts to upgrade the schools came through the National Defense Education Act (NDEA). NDEA was a forerunner of the Elementary-Secondary Education Act (ESEA) which gave even larger amounts of federal aid to the schools and had more direct effects on classroom practices.

Among other things, NDEA-funded institutes provided summer and in-service instruction to teachers of mathematics and science and to guidance counselors. NDEA also provided funds for instructional and library materials. And NDEA provided advanced graduate level fellowships to prepare high levels of technically prepared people who, in turn, could improve the quality of higher education and the preparation of teachers.

Concurrently, the National Science Foundation (NSF) supported workshops, fellowship programs, and curriculum projects aimed at improving instruction in the schools. Of particular importance in the NSF efforts were curriculum projects such as the School Mathematics Study Group (SMSG) which gave rise to the "new math," the Physical Sciences School Curriculum (PSSC), Chemistry Study (CHEMS), the Chemical Bond Approach (CBA) to the study of chemistry, and the Biological Sciences Curriculum Study (BSCS) project. The goals of these projects were to change the content of high school courses and their methods of instruction. With the exception of BSCS, little effort was spent in evaluating their effectiveness and improving the effectiveness of teachers who would use the materials. The wisdom of some of these contributions such as the "new math" has been questioned, but each served to change the curriculum of the schools.

NDEA and the curriculum projects of NSF were the responses of a shocked nation. Although Russia's launching of a satellite before the United States was clearly the result of a political decision, the blame for the "lag" in space technology was placed on the schools. It was commonly believed that schools had failed to teach learners what they needed to know and that their graduates were deficient in technological knowledge. Because it was thought that our country needed more technologically well-prepared people, television commercials proclaimed that "America cannot afford to lose even one of its potentially promising students;" "When your children are ready for college, will college be ready for them? Support the college of your choice."

It is clear that the intention of the Congress was to use young people to save the nation since the opening paragraph of the NDEA act stated, "The Congress hereby finds and declares that the security of the nation requires the fullest development of the mental resources and technical skills of its young men and women."

Pressure groups insisted that schools improve; each group had its own ideas about what would constitute improvement. Subject-matter proficiency was usually their paramount concern. Schools began to respond. They changed curricular content; concentrated more on subject-matter achievement, especially in the sciences and mathematics; departmentalized instruction at earlier grade levels; changed instructional methods; and introduced numerous experimental curriculum projects. Each of these changes was supposed to enhance academic achievement. Each increased the pressure on learners to succeed.

Schools were encouraged to experiment and were assisted in this through funds provided by ESEA, NDEA, NSF, and other federal legislation. Furthermore, schools had no choice other than to experiment, introduce "innovative" procedures and programs, and provide remedial programs even when professional judgment counseled caution. If schools did not apply for and receive grants for federally aided special programs and projects, their administrators in effect committed political suicide. Patrons demanded to know why available resources for improving schools were not being used. Special programs and programs for special children often became the tail which wagged the dog.

Almost without exception, federal aid to the schools has been "categorical" in nature. That is, grants are made for specially designated purposes, not for general aid. Thus schools were forced to concentrate on special aspects of their programs even if such concentration was not needed. In the main, help was provided to do new things or to do things in new ways but not to improve what was already being done. A frequent result was a distortion of curricular emphasis and frustration of school personnel.

Subject-matter excellence became the primary criterion of success for the schools. Its emphasis continues to mount. Storm clouds of student resistence and rebellion appeared in the 1960s and the early 1970s but little attention was given them. The concerns of student leaders were ignored. Students saw themselves as less important than material objects and subject-matter achievement, and believed they were being exploited and depersonalized in efforts to use them for the solution of the nation's problems. Evidence of mounting school violence, vandalism, drug abuse, alcoholism, and mass rejection of long sought-for values did not cause a reexamination of the directions schools were being forced to take. Instead, it was assumed that schools should correct these problems while pressing for higher levels of subject-matter achievement.

Pressures and Problems —

The schools concentrated more and more on subject-matter, and critics clamored for even more. Few people guessed that there might be a relationship between the increased concentration on textbook-centered subject-matter and mounting symptoms of serious problems in school-age youth. Instead, as students' personal and social problems mounted, special resources were developed for treating them. Schools increased the number and type of special education classes and the employment of school psychologists and guidance counselors. Communities increased their support of mental health clinics. Even so, the number of people in need continued to increase.

School vandalism and school violence have become serious matters. Some school systems report a serious decline in the quality of school programs because of them. The Congress became concerned and requested the National Institute of Education (NIE) to investigate vandalism and violence in the schools and to report back [3].

NIE's study showed that vandalism and school violence increased in the late 1960s and the early 1970s to a high level and the increase has leveled off since that time. It showed, also, that the problems are widespread and not limited to urban areas as some believe. Suburban and rural schools suffer from the same problems as do the urban schools.

A particularly surprising finding in the NIE study was that, unlike the early 1970s, the focus of the problem is at the junior high school level rather than the high school level. "Personal violence is most pronounced in junior highs [4]." "The proportion of junior high school students reporting attacks ... [is] ... about twice as great as that of senior high students [5]." There is also a higher percentage of teachers attacked in junior high schools than in senior high schools.

Other factors associated with violence and vandalism include the grade organization of the schools at the junior high level, the size of the school, and whether or not there is a firm, fair system for running the school; that is, are the rules known and firmly and fairly enforced? If the junior high grades are included in a 6-6, an 8-4, or a 1-12 plan of school organization, there is less violence and vandalism than if they exist in separate schools. Likewise, small schools with smaller classes have less violence than large schools with larger classes.

Of particular interest is the NIE finding that teachers' attitudes toward students are related to violence and vandalism. According to NIE, problems are more frequent in schools where students believe their teachers are authoritarian and have a low regard for them. It is equally plausible that teachers hold negative attitudes toward students who are violent or who are vandals. It is also possible that teachers feel that such students need strong control.

NIE's findings in regard to the violence of students and the authoritarianism of their teachers is of particular importance. Teachers believe they must stress academic achievement. They also believe that this goal calls for increased control of students' academic efforts through more dominant teacher behavior. This leads teachers to be seen as authoritarian and resented by students. Thus the attempted solution to the problem of students' lack of technical proficiency may contribute to the rapid increase in school vandalism and violence.

Human Turmoil —

Other problems and symptoms of problems can be added to the list to show that we live in a period of upheaval for schools and for young people. The period is characterized by rapid and extensive moral change, corruption in government, political chicanery, economic inflation, increase in the power of self-centered political lobbyists, the lingering effects of political assassinations, increased centralization of government which has left many people feeling powerless, welfare as a way of life for some, welfare gouging, Medicaid scandals, dual standards in race, sex, and salary matters for members of Congress and for their constituents, and others.

The changing social relationships that have been noted have led to turmoil in the lives of people. We live in a period of rapid change — change which has been so rapid that people are confused about what is right or wrong and have lost sight of guiding philosophical principles. Their worlds have been turned upside down. Many of them long for the past when things seemed to be simpler, less confusing, and the pace of change slower. They long to return to a world which in retrospect seems more satisfying and easier to confront. In such a context, it becomes easy to believe that education has failed, and that if it could be changed to be like it once was, our world would right itself. Obviously, though, education cannot do this. The best it can do is the prepare children to live in the worlds of today and tomorrow.

References

1. I refer to "man" and "he" not because of chauvinism but because in 1950 if anyone looked under the hood of an automobile, it was most likely a man. I might note, too, that in 1950, I would not have had to offer this explanation.

2. Shoben, E. J., Jr. The new student: Implications for personnel work, *CAPS, Capsule*. Fall 1968, Vol. 2, No. 1, p 2.

3. National Institute of Education. Violent Schools—Safe Schools. The Safe School Study Report to the Congress. Vols I and II. February, 1978. *ERIC* ED 149 464 and ED 149 465.

4. National Institute of Education. Violent Schools—Safe Schools. The Safe School Study Report to the Congress. Executive Summary. *ERIC* ED 149 466, p 6.

5. *Ibid*, p 3.

Part II

What the Survey of 124,000 School Age Children in 315 Schools Revealed

Chapter Four

How Students See Themselves and Others

The contemporary scene leads to a prediction that students' perceptions of themselves and of other people must be seriously disturbed. Furthermore, students probably experience severe relationship problems with their teachers, and both they and their parents must hold negative attitudes toward the schools.

Are these predictions valid? If they are, they say much about how education must change. The results of extensive studies which my students and I have conducted show that unfortunately the predictions are correct.

The instruments used in these studies have been described in detail in a book I wrote [1]. They include measures of students' self-concepts and concepts of other people, their attitudes toward school, the types of decision-making relationships students believe they have with their teachers, their perceptions of the qualities of their relationships with their teachers, and parents' attitudes toward the schools.

I have collected a large body of data by using these instruments to help students describe themselves, other students, their schools, and their teachers, and to help parents describe their attitudes toward the schools. A complete description of the methods used in collecting these data and statistical summaries of the data are included in an extensive report in the *Educational Resources Information Center* (ERIC) [2] found in most university libraries.

Some idea of the extensiveness of the survey may make it easier to accept the validity of the conclusions drawn from them. It helps to know, for example, that the self-concept data represent about 119,000 students, while the data which describe the quality of relationships between students and their teachers represent about 124,000 students. These data were collected from students in 315 public, private, and parochial schools located in 12 states spread around the United States. These schools are located in rural areas, small cities, larger cities, and four metropolitan areas. The private schools include the 11 "recently developed" schools David Nevin and I described in *The Schools That Fear Built* [3].

Many of the survey's conclusions are based on the sex or race of the students. Some explanation of why such demographic data were collected seems necessary. Although almost all of the data were collected anonymously, the nature of some of the studies demanded that respondents identify their sex and race. For example, a large portion of the data were collected for the General Assistance Center of The University of Alabama, a federally funded center designed to assist schools in overcoming problems caused by race and sex discrimination. In another instance a large school system was studied to help it formulate school improvement plans to satisfy a federal court desegregation order.

Overall, the data indicate that schools within the same school system differ widely in what their students are like and in how their parents feel about the schools. Students in some schools exhibit problems to a much greater extent than others do. Some schools provide excellent psychological and social climates for students while others have very poor environments. Some of the differences among the schools probably are the results of experiences children have prior to entering school; some are the results of experiences external to the schools during the time they are in school; some probably are the results of the different qualities of experience young people have in school. The data consistently show that schools do make a difference, for better or for worse, in the qualities of the lives of their students.

Students' Self-Concepts —

The self-concept data [4] show that students in the lower grades are more similar to each other than they are in the upper grades and in high school. This is not surprising. As children proceed through school, they become less and less alike in what they know and what is important to them. There should be similar changes in their self-concepts.

A second fact is evident. The older the learners, the more rapidly their self-concepts change. Elementary school children change relatively little from grade 3 through grade 5. On the other hand, students in grades 9-12 change rapidly from one grade to another.

A third trend is that developmental differences are associated first with how students see themselves. After that, while still being concerned with themselves, they become concerned with other people. Finally they are concerned both with themselves and with other people to an extensive degree. The data also show that changes in self-concepts are more rapid in the upper grades and that self-concept development is not complete even in grade 12.

A fourth finding is that when female and male students are compared, impressive differences appear at each grade level. The most significant of these are the different perceptions of male and female students have of what they would like to be and what they think other people would like to be. Without exception and at each of the three school levels, females have significantly higher ideals than males. Many females strive for perfection and hold unrealistically high ideals for themselves and believe that other people have equally high ideals for themselves.

When the self-concept data are examined by the students races, a fifth finding emerges. Differences between black and white students are greater than differences between male and female students. Of the three variables of grade level, sex, and race, the least highly related to differences in self-concepts is school grade level. The most highly related is race.

The most striking differences and probably the most socially and educationally significant differences in black and white students' self-concepts are in their ideals and in what they believe other people idealize. At all three school levels, black students have lower ideals and believe that other people have lower ideals than white students do. Black students say that they do not desire to be as considerate, cooperative, courteous, dependable, faithful, friendly, generous, helpful, honest, kind, polite, sincere, tactful, trustworthy, understanding, and so forth as white students say they want to be. Likewise, black students do not believe that other people want to be as much like these traits as white students do.

These five self-concept findings are of importance in the design of school programs and instructional methods. They show the serious problems involved in teaching students and in promoting healthy self-concept development in school children. They also support the prediction with which this chapter began, that students' self-concepts and their concepts of other people have been seriously disturbed by the climate of the times.

Self Ideal-Self Discrepancy —

The five generalizations just described are important. However, generalizations stemming from comparisons of students' descriptions of themselves and of their ideal selves are even more significant.

People tested with the self-concept measure are presented with lists of trait words. They use these to describe themselves and to describe the self they would like to be, among other things. People who want to be more like the traits than they already are have a positive discrepancy between their self-concepts and their ideal self-concepts (PSID). Those who believe they are already more like the traits than they want to be have negative self ideal-self discrepancies (NSID).

PSID people use the trait words to say, in effect, "We want to be more considerate, courteous, dependable, faithful, honest, trustworthy, and so forth than we presently are." NSID people believe, "We are already more considerate, courteous, dependable, faithful, honest, trustworthy, and so forth than we want to be." A society such as ours needs PSID people to function adequately and to survive. NSID people are poorly equipped to cooperate with other people and to hold positions of responsibility.

Two students and I have made three studies of the effects of self ideal-self discrepancy on school achievement [5]. We found that NSID students are not as highly motivated to do school work as are PSID students and they have more negative attitudes toward school. We also found that teachers assign lower grades to NSID students than to PSID students even when they have equal learning ability and equal achievement.

NSID students desire to be different kinds of people than those valued by their teachers. Because of this they find school less rewarding than PSID students do. They are more likely to be poorly motivated to do school work, and they hold negative attitudes toward school, their teachers, their peers, and other people. They reject school because they feel "picked on" and because teachers insist that their values and attitudes are not desirable. They do not want to be like the students who are considered ideal by most teachers. Their values bring them into automatic conflict with their teachers. They reject teachers, schools, and learning.

The large data base previously described [2] shows that the numbers of NSID students in school today is appalling. In grades 3-5, their percentage is at its lowest level. It averages about 7 per cent. In grade 6, it jumps to more than 30 per cent. Thus in grade 6 almost one-third of the students believe they are already more like the traits on the self-concept test than they want to be.

The percentages of NSID students declines continuously from grade 6 through grade 12 where it averages about 6 per cent. Quite likely most of this change is a result of NSID students dropping out of school. But there is also the frightening possibility, supported by some accumulating evidence, that these middle grade NSID students represent the beginning of a surge of such students who will change the percentages in the high schools when they arrive there. Quite possibly, high schools will show discouragingly large percentages of NSID students in the near future.

In every grade the percentage of NSID students who are male is higher than the percentage who are female. The difference between black and white students is even greater. In grades 6-8, 42 per cent of the black students and 13 per cent of the white students are NSID. In grade 6, 52 per cent of the black students are NSID while only 16 per cent of the white students are NSID. In grades 6-8, there is a wholesale rejection by black students of traits such as those measured by the self-concept test; and although the rejection rate is much lower for white students, it is still a matter for considerable concern.

No wonder many middle school and junior high school teachers report that their schools are jungles! The NIE study of violence and vandalism described earlier is more understandable on the basis of these data. Students who reject traits such as considerate, cooperative, helpful, honest, sincere, trustworthy, and other similar ones are poorly equipped to function in our society. Our schools must be changed so that students can develop the values they will need for success and satisfaction in life and for the continued existence of our society.

Personality Groups —

The self-concept test also yields a descriptive measure by which people can be categorized into personality groups. The differences in the groups depend on how the members see their worth and the worth of other people. People can see themselves as worthwhile or not worthwhile. They can also see other people the same way. Thus the four groups describe themselves as:

++"I am worthwhile and so are other people,"

-+"I am not worthwhile but other people are,"

+-"I am worthwhile but other people are not,"

-- "I am not worthwhile and neither are other people."

For shorthand purposes, the four groups can be designated as + +, - +, + -, or - -. The first + or - shows that people feel worthwhile or not worthwhile.

These four groups of people can be ranked in order of psychological health. From most to least healthy, the groups are + +, - +, + -, and - -. Considerable research has been done to learn more about the personal characteristics of these groups of people [References 6-11]. This research shows that it is important for school experiences to assert positive influences to help students become + + people. The four groups have distinctive personality characteristics which vitally affect their ability to relate to other people, their personal satisfaction in life, and their success.

The data from the large survey already described [2] show that students move from the more positive categories to the less positive ones as they progress through school. This is shown in the table below:

| | Percentages of Students in Each Category | | | |
	++	-+	+-	--
Grades 3-5	34.5	29.4	24.4	11.8
Grades 6-8	20.1	26.4	31.4	22.1
Grades 9-12	15.9	22.0	40.8	21.3

From grades 3-5 through grades 9-12, there is a steady decline in + +, a smaller decline in - +, and a steady increase in + - -- increases from grades 3-5 to grades 6-8 and remains at a high percentage in grades 9-12. These facts mean that as students move through school there are progressive negative changes in the way they see themselves and other people. The data support the assertion of an "I" or "me" generation and show that the percentages of "I" or "me" people (+ -) increases from grade level to grade level. About two of every five high school students have an egocentric frame of reference.

Students in the data base were subdivided into male and

female groups and black and white groups. Examination of the data shows that differences are present in each of the divisions but the most significant differences are between black and white students.

In grades 3-5, about 40 per cent of the black children are + + while 30 per cent of the white children are in this group. The reverse is true in grades 6 through 8. In grades 9-12, though, the percentages of + + black and white students is about equal and a greater percentage of black students are + + than in grades 6-8. At each of the three school levels there are more – + white students than black students and more + – black students than white students.

These data tell at least four things. First, black students do not suffer as much from inadequate self-concepts in grades 3-5 as white students do. Second, when there are disturbances in perceptions of self and other people, the youth of the two races react differently. White students more frequently question their own worth, while black students more frequently question the worth of other people. Another way of saying this is that at each school level, black students are more defensive in their interpersonal relationships than are white students, and they increase in defensiveness at each of the three school levels. White students tend to blame themselves for their problems and shortcomings; black students tend to blame other people.

Third, these data show that more rapid deterioration in attitudes toward self and toward other people occurs for black children after grade 5 than for white children. And fourth, the data suggest that + + black children do not drop out of school as frequently as the other three groups of black children.

The data make it clear that during their school years more serious changes in attitudes toward self and toward other people occur for black children than for white children. From this it can be inferred that black children find school and/or other aspects of maturing more frustrating than do white students. The data, of course, do not tell why this is.

It is not possible to assess responsibility for what is happening to children's feelings of self worth and worth of other people during their school years. It may be that schools are not being successful in developing these characteristics in either black or white children, or it may be that schools are not successful in overcoming the negative effects of the out-of-school experiences children have. Perhaps both in-school and out-of-school experiences work together to produce the negative effects.

The Importance of Self-Concepts —

The self-concept data show that significant, highly negative changes occur in perceptions of self and perceptions of other people as children mature and develop. The changes show that a serious situation exists: the older children become, the less favorably they see themselves and other people, the more defensive they become, and the less they idealize values which are important for human existence and for survival.

A warning is necessary. The way the data were collected and analyzed tends to associate the negative self-concept changes with school experiences. If the data had been collected and analyzed by age groups instead of grade groups, the conclusions would have been identical but would more likely have been associated with age than with school grade.

There is no evidence to prove that the described negative changes are the result of school experiences. Perhaps the changes would be more widespread and negative if the students had not attended school. It could be that the negative changes are the results of experiences students have with their peers, in their homes, or in their communities. One fact is clear. Students in some schools hold much more positive perceptions of themselves and of other people than children in comparable schools. This suggests that some schools have more positive influences on the development of children than others and some have more negative influences. It is also possible that some communities have more positive effects (or less negative ones) on children than others.

It is impossible to factor out the effects of schooling and say that schools are either the cause of the negative changes or that they prevent more negative changes from occurring. On the other hand, schools are responsible for doing what they can to prevent or reverse the described negative self-concept trends. Clearly, they are not now doing this successfully.

What is certain is this: The people who clamor the loudest for changes in the schools also take the position that students' ability to relate successfully to other people, their sense of values, their personal welfare, and other important aspects of their lives are not rightful concerns of the schools. These people argue that schools should attend only to what they believe is the purpose of schools — the teaching of subject-matter — and should ignore all other aspects of students' development. The self-concept data refute such an argument. Young people's lives are being seriously impaired by what is happening to them in the process of growing up.

References

1. Bills, R. E. *A System for Assessing Affectivity.* University: The University of Alabama Press, 1975.
2. Bills, R. E. Summary Data and Interpretations: A System for Assessing Affectivity, *ERIC* ED 166 243.
3. Nevin, D. & Bills, R. E. *The Schools That Fear Built.* Washington: Acropolis Books Ltd., 1976.
4. These data were collected by use of The Index of Adjustment and Values. For a description of this instrument see reference #1, above.
5. Finch, J. D., Finch, C. Bills, & Bills, R. E. Values and school achievement. *Proceedings: Mid-South Educational Research Association.* November 11, 1972, p 62-63.
6. Bills, R. E. A comparison of scores on the Index of Adjustment and Values with behavior in level of aspiration tasks. *Journal of Consulting Psychology,* 1953, 17, 206-212.
7. Bills, R. E. Rorschach characteristics of persons scoring high and low in acceptance of self. *Journal of Consulting Psychology,* 1953, 17, 36-38.
8. Bills, R. E. *A System for Assessing Affectivity.* University: The University of Alabama Press, 1975.
9. Bills, R. E. Acceptance of self as measured by interviews and The Index of Adjustment and Values. *Journal of Consulting Psychology,* 1954, 18, p 22.
10. Bills, R. E. Self concepts and Rorschach signs of depression. *Journal of Consulting Psychology,* 1954, 18, 135-137.
11. Bills, R. E. *About People and Teaching.* Lexington: University of Kentucky Bureau of School Services, 1955.

Chapter Five

Students Look at Teachers:
What They See and What They Want

Two factors in the relationships of students and teachers influence the quality and importance of what students learn. The first of these is the type of decision-making processes existing in classrooms. The second is the quality of the personal relationships students experience with their teachers. Where these are optimal, students learn to be responsible for themselves, learn how to make important decisions, become open to the personal meanings of experience, and can profit from new experience. They can behave intelligently.

Classroom Decision-Making

Information in the data base [1] about students' perceptions of decision-making processes in their classrooms was collected by means of a 27-item multiple-choice instrument [2]. Students answer the question, "Who is making the decisions in this classroom?" Three types of alternatives are possible for each item: 1) the teacher makes the decision, 2) the teacher and the students make the decision together, and 3) the students make the decision by themselves.

Teachers have several decision-making options. They can act as if students cannot make decisions for themselves, in which case the teacher makes the decisions for them. Or teachers may believe that students can make wise choices if they are given adequate guidance. It also is possible for teachers to believe that students are capable of making wise decisions without help in a large variety of circumstances. Most teachers believe that an important outcome of education is increased decision-making ability. Few give students many opportunities to make decisions, though. They seem to believe their job is to inform students because informed people can make adequate decisions for themselves. Too, teachers who feel responsible for what is learned in their classrooms make many decisions for students.

My research shows that there is an optimal balance in the making of classroom decisions. This may be expressed as a ratio of 1:2:1, which means that for each decision a teacher makes *for* students, two decisions are made by the students *and* their teacher in interaction, and one is made by students for themselves.

Effective teachers give students as much time as possible to explore alternatives and to help in making decisions. When teachers can develop interactive decision-making processes in their classrooms, students discover personal meaning in what is to be learned and become involved in learning it. In classrooms where interactive decision-making is practiced, student morale is high.

Interestingly, when the amount of student-made decisions is unusually high in a classroom, students are not necessarily being given opportunities. Instead, they may be being ignored. This situation occurs most often when teachers are apprehensive and believe they should "let sleeping dogs lie." When students who cause problems are not disturbing other students, why change things?

Students feel like prisoners in their classrooms if teachers make too many decisions for them. If teachers leave too many decisions for students to make by themselves, many will be anxious. Most students learn best when a warm, understanding teacher works with them to help them make decisions which both the teacher and the students believe are good ones.

Grade Level and Decision-Making —

The data base [1] contains scores representing the decision-making perceptions of over 100,000 students in grades 4-12. Overall, these data show that teachers make 43 per cent of the decisions, another 38 per cent are made by teachers in inter-action with students, and 19 per cent are made by the students. This means that teachers make more decisions for students than with them, and they make more than twice as many decisions for them as they permit students to make for them-selves. In comparison with the optimal ratio of 1:2:1, the average classroom is far too teacher-dominated.

In grades 3 through 6, teachers make about as many decisions for students as they make with them. Beginning at grade 7, though, the amount of teacher-made decisions increases rapidly and the amount of interactive decision-making decreases slightly. The percentage of student-made decisions is low at each grade level, and from grade 4 through grade 12 there is a gradual decline.

The further students progress in school, the less opportunity they have to help in making decisions or to make decisions for themselves. This does not augur well for students' futures. The ability to make good decisions for oneself rests upon opportunities to practice decision-making and to learn to live with the consequences.

As children proceed through school and supposedly learn and mature, they are given less and less opportunity to make decisions for themselves. This is frustrating for them. It is no less frustrating for their teachers. Teachers find themselves in a system which tells them what must be taught and when it must be taught — a system centered around textbooks rather than around the interests and concerns of children. They often find themselves ignoring their own feelings and beliefs about how much children should enter the decision-making process in order to "cover" the required amount of subject-matter.

When students are robbed of opportunities for making decisions for themselves, they become frustrated and hostile. The older they become, the more frustrating such denials become. From almost any point of view, it makes sense to give students more responsibility for themselves as they mature. But schools provide less opportunity because of their textbook-centered approach to subject-matter and their "lock step" curricula. Children in the lower grades have more opportunity to make decisions for themselves than they will ever have at any subsequent time in their school experience.

Sex and Decision-Making —

Different decision-making relationships occur between boys and teachers and girls and teachers. Boys are more dominated by their teachers than are girls. Girls interact more with their teachers in the making of decisions than do boys. And boys more often make decisions for themselves, which probably means that boys are ignored more by their teachers than are girls.

In each of the grades, boys report more teacher-made decisions, fewer interactive decisions, and more student-made decisions than do girls. To an important degree, teachers are too busy interacting with girls to do more than dictate to boys or ignore them. Thus, girls enjoy better decision-making relationships with their teachers than boys do.

Race and Decision-Making —

As seen through the eyes of students, both black and white students are subject to more teacher-made decisions than to interactive decisions. Black children, however, report less teacher domination at each grade level than do white children. Furthermore, black children after grade 6 report a higher level of interaction with their teachers than is reported by white children.

Significant differences occur also in perceptions of the amount of decisions both black and white students make for themselves. Both groups report significant declines from grade 4 through grade 12, but black students in each grade report that they make more decisions by themselves than are reported by white students. Again, this may only indicate that black students are ignored more than white students are.

These comparisons must be interpreted with caution. Black children more often come from adult-dominated homes than do white children. One consequence of this domination may be that, given equal amounts of domination by a teacher, black students report less domination than white students. This presents problems for teachers. What may be too harsh treatment for some students may be too lenient for others.

School Violence and Decision-Making —

Reference has been made to the findings of the study of school violence and vandalism by the National Institute of Education [3, 4], that teachers' attitudes toward students are related to violence and vandalism. According to that study, violence and vandalism are more frequent in schools where teachers are viewed by their students as authoritarian and having a low regard for the worth of students. The decision-making data are relevant to the NIE findings.

Dennis Barbakow, one of my students, made a study of violence in a southern metropolitan school system [5]. That school system was one of the systems which contributed to the data base [1]. At a later date another student, John Fancher, correlated Barbakow's violence scores for the schools in the system with their scores on the decision-making measure.

Fancher found that at the high school level there was no significant correlation between the degrees of violence of the schools and the decision-making measurements. In grades 4-8, however, he found that in schools where the levels of interactive decision-making is high, the amount of violence is low. This, of course, does not say which causes which. It may be that teachers are less able to be interactive with violent children, or it may be that where teachers are interactive children are less violent. Correlational studies can never sort out cause and effect; the study does not tell us if we need more interactive teachers or less violent students. We probably need some of each. It is certain, though, that we cannot make violent students less violent by dominating them.

Summary of Decision-Making Processes —

The data show that in decision-making processes, students experience more teacher domination than interaction and that teacher domination increases grade by grade while interaction decreases. Teachers dominate boys more than girls at all school levels, especially after grade 6. Teachers interact more with girls than with boys. They also interact more with black students than with white, although the interaction of teachers is less closely associated with the races of the students than with their sexes. Teachers interact with white girls to such a great degree that there is little opportunity left for the girls to make decisions for themselves.

Teacher-Student Relationships

The data bank also contains information about the qualities of relationships between teachers and their students. These data were collected by use of an instrument which students complete to describe the qualities of the relationships they believe exist between them and their teachers [6].

Four qualities are involved. Taken together, these are the qualities teachers need to help students become open to the meanings of their experiences and to remain open to them. Open people are creative and imaginative and able to use their knowledge and experience to behave intelligently. Thus teachers who have these four qualities are able to provide their students with relationships helpful to them in their intellectual development. The four qualities are *level of regard, empathic understanding, unconditionality of regard,* and *congruence.*

Level of regard is the degree to which teachers regard students as worthwhile people. The higher the level of regard, the more the teachers believe the students have worth as people.

Empathic understanding is a measure of teachers' ability to understand students as the students understand themselves. It is the quality referred to when someone speaks of "walking around in another person's shoes."

Unconditionality of regard is related to the "price" teachers place on their regard for students. Do the teachers regard them as important regardless of how they behave, dress, live, and so forth? Or do the teachers regard the sons and daughters of rich parents and community leaders as more important than those of poor people and others with little influence? Teachers who are unconditional in their regard believe that all young people have equal worth. The unconditionally regarding teacher believes that students have worth even though they may behave in unacceptable ways.

Congruence is a measure of the degree to which students believe that what their teachers are thinking or feeling and what they are doing are identical. Teachers who say one thing and who seem to think or feel another are seen as incongruent by students.

The Helpful Person —

Helpful people (for example, parents and friends and sometimes clergymen, physicians, and others) are people who hold a high level of regard for us, have an emphathic understanding of what it is to be like us, are unconditional in their regard for us, and are congruent in their relationships with us. If teachers are seen by students as being positively and unconditionally regarding, being empathic, and behaving congruently in their relationships, the teachers are helpful people.

Being a helpful person implies being able to create a psychological climate in which other people can be themselves and lower their defenses. When people lower their defenses, more of their experience becomes available to them in an undistorted manner and they become more aware of its personal meanings.

Only that experience which is personally meaningful to us affects our behavior. If what is learned in school is to affect the behavior of students, they must see its personal meaning for them. Teachers who are seen by students as unconditionally positive, empathic, and congruent help them to become less defensive, have more undistorted experience with personal meanings more readily available, and base their behavior on a broader base of experience. In such a relationship, students examine the personal meaning of new experience and are changed by it.

Openness and Helping Relationships —

Frank Emmerling, a student of mine, studied the relationship between teachers' personal qualities and the qualities of the relationships they afford students [7]. Emmerling measured the openness to experience of teachers enrolled in a summer workshop at a university campus. He predicted that teachers who are more open to experience have relationship qualities which enable their students to become more open to their experience. His predictions were based on the following understandings: open teachers are less anxious in dealing with other people; they tend to see problems as challenges rather than threats; they sometimes blame themselves for their failures and sometimes blame other people or circumstances; they center their concerns on what they can do about solving their problems rather than on placing blame; and they look to the future for solutions to problems rather than the past. He predicted that the relationships open teachers provide students are more helpful than those less open teachers provide.

During the ensuing year, Emmerling visited randomly selected classrooms of these teachers. The students in these classes were asked to complete an instrument to describe relationships with the teachers. The more open teachers were described by their students as having a higher level of regard, more empathic understanding, more unconditionality of regard, and more congruence than those who were less open.

Few teacher preparation programs attempt to help teachers become more open to their experience. Instead, many features of preparation programs, for example student teaching, threaten teachers in training. Classrooms are threatening even to experienced teachers. It is threatening to be responsible for the intellectual development of as many students as teachers have. No wonder they become defensive! Unfortunately, defensive teachers are less able to be positive and unconditional in their expression of regard, to be empathic, and to be congruent than less defensive ones. They and their students suffer.

Because of the threats they face, it is not surprising to discover that teachers do not score high on any of the relationship qualities. They score higher on liking students and being honest with them than on understanding them as they understand themselves and accepting them unconditionally. In our culture, it is difficult for adults to be unconditional in their expressions of regard for young people. Young people do not behave as adults think they should, and adults show their displeasure. Usually this displeasure is seen by young people as a lack of regard for them as people, not as disapproval of their behavior. In many instances, parents and teachers *do* threaten to withhold love and/or regard unless the children behave as they desire.

Grade Level and Relationship Qualities —

The amounts of unconditionality of regard and congruence that students describe their teachers as having are related to students' grade levels. The older the students, the more honest and less conditional they believe their teachers are in relationships with them. Teachers apparently find it easier to relax their demands on older students and to be more honest with them.

The relationships between level of regard and empathic understanding and grade level are not so simple. Although neither level of regard nor empathic understanding are high in grade 6, there is a decline through grade 8 and then only a small improvement in succeeding grades.

The decline in level of regard and empathic understanding from grade 6 through grade 8 reinforces what was said earlier. The NIE study [3, 4] shows that violence and vandalism are most prevelant in the middle grades. Barbakow's study [5] also shows that violence and vandalism are more frequent in the upper grades of elementary schools (grades 6 to 8). No doubt teachers have at least to a degree the low level of regard and empathic understanding which teachers in grades 6-8 are described as having. But how much of this is the result of how students behave, how much the cause? Or how much of it is because young people at this grade level are so imbued with their own sense of importance that they are unable to sense the qualities of the relationships teachers are offering them? These questions are unanswerable at present.

Sex and Relationship Qualities —

Changes in the four relationship characteristics for both boys and girls as they move from grade to grade closely resemble those described for decision-making relationships. Unconditionally of regard and congruence, although never high, gradually improve from grade 6 through grade 12 for both boys and girls. Level of regard and empathic understanding show the same "dip" in grades 6-8 and then rise from grade 9-12 for both boys and girls.

Girls describe better relationships with their teachers at each grade level than do boys. In all grades, teachers have a higher level of regard for girls, are more empathically understanding of girls, are less conditional in the expression of their regard for girls, and are more honest with girls.

There probably are many reasons for this bias. Research shows that when girls enter school, they are able to engage in sustained activities for longer periods of time than boys. It also shows that girls are less restless and more interested in the kinds of tasks teachers assign. When they enter school, girls are more interested in abstract things such as reading and arithmetic than boys are. Boys are more interested in the manipulation of objects and in differences and similarities among physical objects — characteristics which enable them to excel in science and mathematics in later grades. As a consequence, girls are easier to work with in elementary grades than are boys, and girls give teachers less trouble than boys do.

As a consequence of such attributes, boys are more frequently classified as hyperactive and as having learning problems. Boys learn to read more slowly than girls and are more often classed as dyslexic [8]. Thus girls are easier to work with in school and are a greater source of satisfaction for their teachers. Not only is it easier to provide girls with helpful relationships but under the curricular demands of the schools, it may be more possible to provide girls with such relationships than to provide them to boys.

Race and Relationship Qualities —

Almost without exception, at each grade level the qualities of relationships between teachers and their white students are superior to the qualities black students see in their teachers. This is true regardless of whether the teachers are black or white. However, with the exception of congruence, the differences between the races are relatively small, in most instances smaller than the differences between the perceptions of girls and boys. Congruence scores show a greater difference between black and white students than between girls and boys. Thus differences in how students see their teachers' level of regard, empathic understanding, and unconditionality of regard are more dependent on the sexes of the students than their races; the difference in congruence is more dependent on the students' races.

Relationship Inventory Summary —

The average student does not have desirable relationships with teachers. Teachers find it easier to like students and be honest with them than to understand them or to be unconditional in their regard for them.

Girls enjoy better relationships with their teachers than boys do, and white students describe better relationships with their teachers than black students do. Differences in relationships which are associated with race are less significant than those associated with sex with the exception of congruence.

Students, on the average, describe better relationship qualities with black teachers than with white teachers. However, students have better qualities of relationships with teachers of the same race than with teachers of the other race.

The relationship and decision-making data show that students differ widely from each other. Furthermore, important differences exist between the descriptions given by the two sexes and black and white students. A similar conclusion was stated for the self-concept data. These differences emphasize the difficulties present in teaching the heterogeneous groups most teachers must teach. They also emphasize the need for teachers to be concerned for what is happening to boys and girls in their classrooms and for their development in general. They suggest a need for close interaction between students and teachers to maximize opportunities for helpful relationships.

References

1. Bills, R. E. Summary Data and Interpretations: A System for Assessing Affectivity. *ERIC* ED 166 243.

2. See Locus of Responsibility Scale in R. E. Bills, *A System for Assessing Affectivity.* University: The University of Alabama Press, 1975.

3. National Institute of Education. Violent Schools—Safe Schools. The Safe School Study Report to the Congress. Vols. I and II. February 1978. *ERIC* ED 149 464 and ED 149 465.

4. National Institute of Education. Violent Schools—Safe Schools. The Safe School Study Report to the Congress. Executive Summary. *ERIC* ED 149 466.

5. Barbakow, D. R. *A Study of Violence in a Southern Metropolitan School System.* The University of Alabama, unpublished doctoral dissertation, 1976.

6. See Relationship Inventory in R. E. Bills, *A System for Assessing Affectivity.* University: The University of Alabama Press, 1975.

7. Emmerling, F. C. *A Study of the Relationships Between Personality Characteristics of Classroom Teachers and Pupil Percepts of these Teachers.* Auburn University, unpublished doctoral dissertation, 1961.

8. Dyslexia is an interesting phenomenon introduced into schools in recent years. It means only that a child has difficulty in reading, but usually far more meaning is read into it; and it is believed to be a cause of poor reading instead of being a word which means poor reading ability.

Chapter Six

How Students
and Parents
Feel About School

The negative conclusions growing from the self-concept, decision-making, and interpersonal relationship data lead to a prediction that students and their parents do not feel positively about the schools. The data support the expectation.

How Students Feel About School

The data base contains descriptions of students' attitudes toward school collected by a 50 item true-false instrument [1]. These data were examined in a number of ways. One of these was by the students' grade level in school.

Grade Level and School Attitudes —

The grade level data show that the further people go in school, the less positively they feel about it. In grade 4, pupils hold strong positive attitudes toward school. From grade 4 through grade 10, however, there is a sharp negative change. There is only slight improvement in their attitudes in grades 11 and 12, which for most students is above compulsory attendance age. In grade 10, the average student holds a "neutral" attitude toward school — that is, about half of the attitude responses are positive and half are negative. This also means that about half of the students in grade 10 hold negative attitudes toward their schools.

These changes in attitude with changes in grade are not difficult to understand. Most children enter school with positive attitudes. They are excited about this new experience. Their teachers help them to maintain their excitement and eagerness to learn by delegating responsibility to them, listening carefully to their communications, coordinating instruction with their readiness for it, and many other means. The children begin to learn what they believe are important things, and they feel positively about what is happening to them.

In grade 4 a remarkable change begins to occur in the instructional process. Schools begin to define more precisely what, when, and how much students must learn by the end of each school year. This is readily apparent in those schools which use departmentalized instruction. Many middle schools (grades 5-8) departmentalize all of their instruction, and some schools use departmentalized instruction below grade 5.

Teachers begin to feel pressures to "cover" the material described in the curriculum so that the pupils will be prepared for the next grade. What makes this change remarkable is the fact that to this point in school, children have been making excellent progress. Teachers have helped them find meaning in what they are learning, considered their readiness for new tasks before beginning them, grouped them to tailor instruction to their levels of learning and readiness, and done other things to accommodate instruction to children's individual learning needs, states of readiness, and rates of learning.

The reversal of concern beginning in grade 4 causes problems for many youngsters. When children enter first grade, their teachers expect them to differ from each other in terms of how much they know and how ready they are to learn what is being taught. Teachers know that some pupils are more ready to learn and will learn more rapidly than others. If pupils have good teachers, they will differ more from each other at the end of the first grade than they did at the beginning. They become even more different from each other in the second grade, and, as pointed out previously, with good instruction they differ more at the end of each school year.

When teachers feel pressures to make all children achieve equally, they begin to offer the same instruction in the same way to all of them. Even though the children have grown less and less alike, teachers treat them as if they were identical. By the time they reach grade 6 or grade 7 in most schools, all students are given the same assignments and required to meet the same standards.

Some schools attempt to avoid such "lock step" instruction by using teaching methods which supposedly individualize instruction. But even though instruction is individualized, the goals are not. All of the students are expected to arrive at the same place at the same time. Even though students may be working at their top levels, many fall further and further behind and are labeled failures. The imposition of adult needs on students is probably worst where schools use behavioral objectives. In such cases, the effectiveness of teaching is gauged by the degree to which students' behavior matches predetermined criteria arbitrarily decided upon by those in authority without consultation with students or consideration of individual students' abilities. When such things happen to learners, school is no longer exciting and need-fulfilling. It is a source of frustration.

The longer students remain in classrooms in which they do not feel important and in which arbitrary standards are imposed on them, and the less opportunity students have to engage in interactive decision-making, the more negatively they feel about themselves and other people and the poorer are their relationships with their teachers. Naturally, they develop more and more negative feelings about school and begin to live for the time when they no longer will be compelled to attend. Many of them drop out after grade 10, in spirit if not in reality.

Attitude Factors —

The relationships students have with teachers is directly related to the students' attitudes toward school. Another of my students, Charles Minder, studied the responses of students to the school attitude measure [2]. He found that four factors are present in students' descriptions of their schools. The first factor is a negative attitude students hold toward *some* teachers. A second is a positive attitude toward selected aspects of schools. The third factor is a positive attitude students have toward *most* of the teachers and their school in general. The fourth is a negative attitude toward the compulsory and impersonal aspects of school.

Minder's study supports the assertions made in the immediately preceding section. Students' negative attitudes toward school are the results of the relationships they experience with some teachers and the compulsory and impersonal aspects of schooling. Students like most of their teachers and, in general, they like their schools. They dislike how some teachers treat them and how some aspects of schooling depersonalize them.

Attitudes and Decision-Making —

Charles Houston, also one of my students, used the data base to study the relationship between students' attitudes toward school and decision-making relationships with teachers [3]. His results indicate that when teachers dominate the decision-making process, students feel less positively about their schools. However, when teachers are more interactive than dominating, students feel more positively about school. Furthermore, the more teachers allow students to make decisions for themselves, the more positively the students feel about their schools. Houston's results parallel those of the NIE study of violence and lend further support to the assertions about the negative consequences of changes in teaching styles and objectives which begin about grade 4.

Responses of Students —

Students' feelings about school can be illustrated by examining the responses to the school attitude measure given in a survey of a large school system. These results summarize the anonymous responses of almost 10,000 students in grades 4-12.

Item 1 of the measure says, "I am learning things in school which help me now." Almost 91 per cent said this statement was true. They also responded in a positive manner to items such as these:

Statement	Percentage of Students Who Agree
In general, I like my teachers.	83.0
Most of the teachers try to be fair in dealing with the students.	82.5
Most of the teachers are fair in their criticism of my work.	79.6
Most of the teachers are pleasant and cheerful most of the time.	76.8
Our teachers are interested in us.	75.8
My teachers are honest with me.	75.2
My teachers usually have a good sense of humor.	74.6
My teachers like me.	71.4
The students are given a square deal in most of the school activities.	70.9
My teachers try to understand me.	67.9

If students give positive answers to such items on the school attitude measure, how can it be concluded that they hold negative attitudes toward their schools? The answer is these positive responses are more than outweighed by negative ones, and that all teachers do some things which "turn students off." Some teachers have characteristics which are especially galling.

In addition, there are some things about the structure of the curriculum which are unacceptable to students.

Look at some of the negative attitudes expressed in the responses listed below by the same group of students who gave the positive responses:

Statement	Percentage of Students Who Agree
Some of the women teachers show favoritism toward boys in their classes.	77.1
Some of the teachers assign unreasonable amounts of homework.	66.0
Some of my classes are so uninteresting that I cannot do my best work.	65.2
Some of the men teachers show favoritism toward girls in their classes.	65.2
Our teachers do not pay enough attention to what we are interested in.	64.7
Some of my courses are extremely boring.	63.2
Some of the teachers act as if they want the students to be afraid of them.	61.6
The teachers pick on some of the kids.	61.0
Some of the teachers act as if they want the students to feel embarrassed.	59.9
Some of my teachers do not grade fairly.	50.5
Some of the teachers are lazy.	50.0
Too many of our teachers have pets.	49.6

It should be emphasized that the school system in which these responses were collected is not different from most other school systems. The similarity of students' responses from one school system to another is astonishingly high.

From the list of responses, it is obvious that students are not afraid to express themselves. They believe that all teachers do some unacceptable things and that some aspects of schooling are unacceptable. The source of most of their negative attitudes toward their schools are relationships with some of their teachers.

These responses to the school attitude measure plus others not listed show that it is not teachers alone who are responsible for students' negative attitudes toward school. Young people find school boring and their classes sometimes so uninteresting that they cannot do their best work.

What happens to children before grade 4 or 5 promotes positive attitudes toward school; what happens in later grades promotes less positive attitudes.

Sex and Feelings About School —

At each grade level, girls hold less negative attitudes toward school than boys do. This is not surprising in light of their decision-making relationships and the quality of their inter-personal relationships with teachers. The difference in feelings about school held by boys and girls is greatest in the middle grade range, particularly in grades 5 and 6, although it is sub-stantial for most of the grades.

When the school attitude scores for all students, for girls, and for boys are compared grade by grade, the distributions are essentially the same. The major difference is that boys show more negative attitudes at each grade level than girls do.

Sex and Race and Feelings About Schools —

Although changes in feelings about school from grade to grade for each of the four race-sex groups differ significantly from each other, each is similar to the pattern for the total group and to those for boys and girls. Thus, the pattern of change from grade to grade is similar for each group although some groups have more negative feelings than others do.

At each grade level, white girls have more positive feelings about school than the other three groups. This is quite likely the result of the more desirable decision-making and interpersonal relationships which girls have with their teachers. It is also possible that because white girls feel more positively toward school, their teachers find them easier to work with and thus to have more favorable relationships with them. Perhaps both of these alternatives operate at the same time and reinforce each other.

The poorest attitudes toward school are held by white boys. Black girls and black boys differ little from each other. Their attitudes fall between those of white girls and white boys.

Parents' Beliefs About School

The Parent Inventory [4], a 35-item multiple-choice instrument, was sent to students' homes to collect information about parents' attitudes and opinions for the data base. Parents are asked to complete the instrument for each school level in which they have a child or children. School levels are divided into grades 1-3, 4-6, 7-9, and 10-12. The Parent Inventory is scored to give an attitude score. In addition, the parents' responses are tabulated.

Parents' Attitudes and School Level —

Parents do not hold strong positive attitudes toward the schools at any school level. Furthermore, their attitudes become less positive as their children progress from one grade level to another. On the basis of students' attitudes toward school, this is understandable. Parents form their attitudes in part from information they receive from their children, from their recall of their own school experiences, and from the media. In the case of recall, parents' attitudes probably are more closely associated with their high school experiences than with their elementary school experiences, making the attitudes more negative.

The data show that the higher the children are in school, the less positive are the attitudes of their parents. Quite likely this is because parents have unrealistically high hopes for what schools can do to help their children. Instead of achieving these, they see the developing negative attitudes of their children toward the schools and the other negative changes already discussed. As a consequence, parents react negatively. Their views are reinforced by critics of the schools who make good news stories and some politicians who use the schools as a vehicle for being elected to office.

Attitudes of Black and White Parents —

When parents' attitudes are examined by school level and by parents' races, it is seen that differences in attitudes across the grade levels are not the same for black and white parents. Black parents of children in grades 1-3 feel more positively toward the schools than white parents at this same level although the difference is not large. At each succeeding grade level, white parents' attitudes toward the schools are less positive. There is a somewhat less regular change for black parents, but at each of the four school levels the average attitude score of white parents is less positive than that of black parents. Since black parents hold more favorable attitudes toward the schools than do white parents, in this respect parents and their children are alike.

Parents' Goals for Schools —

In responding to the Parent Inventory, parents rank goals for the schools in terms of the emphases they believe should be given them. The goals include such things as: help children decide whether or not to go to college; help children acquire good manners, poise, personal appearance, and self-confidence; help children discover their vocational interests and abilities; help children develop work habits and study skills; help pupils learn to control their conduct; help children distinguish right from wrong and guide their actions accordingly; stress the teaching of the basic school subjects; and help students learn how to take independent action.

The survey results show that parents' opinions about the schools do not agree with each other. They also do not agree with some of the critics of the schools who believe that the major problem is that schools do not stress the teaching of basic school subjects. A large majority of parents believe that schools should teach the basic subjects but they also believe the schools should do much more. They are concerned, for example, about their children's moral, vocational, and personal development.

Parents vary widely in the type of moral development they desire for their children. Some believe that schools should not teach morality. Others believe moral development is more important than basic school subjects. Some parents want enough morality taught that their children can get along well with other people and avoid serious problems. Others want the schools to reinforce the moral training of their churches.

About 57 per cent of the parents believe that their children need more help on their homework. They also believe the schools should provide it, even though by definition homework is something done at home. More than one in ten has no opinion about how much help their children need. They are only a small part of the group which is poorly informed about where their children are and how much time they spend on their school work. About one-fourth of the parents believe too little homework is required, and only about one parent in ten believes that the amount of homework is entirely too much.

When parents are asked how much time their children spend on their homework each day, about 20 per cent say they spend less than half an hour, 30 per cent say they spend less than one hour, another 30 per cent report more than two hours each day, and over 15 per cent say they do not know how much time their children spend on their homework. The situation may even be worse. Some parents who say they know how much time their children spend in studying really do not know. One reason why students are not learning as much in school as their parents would like is apparent; they are not spending much time on their studies.

When parents are asked about the amount of help their schools provide students in things such as solving personal and social problems and in deciding on their future work, only about 18 per cent believe that the schools give sufficient help. Over 25 per cent believe that the schools should provide more help. Almost 40 per cent state that they do not know how much help is provided. Less than 10 per cent believe that the schools should not offer help in these areas.

School personnel should be shocked by the 40 per cent of the parents who have no idea about the amount of help school children are provided for solving personal and social problems. All schools provide considerable help through classroom teachers and special personnel, for example, guidance counselors and school psychologists. The schools' efforts should be communicated to parents. Parents also are asked their opinions about the amount of time that should be spent teaching "the basics." About 40 per cent believe the emphases are about right; 22 per cent believe the schools do not concentrate enough on them; and 18 per cent believe there is so much concentration on the basics that the schools cannot offer sufficient chance for children's creativity. More than 16 per cent of the parents have no opinion on this item. The 22 per cent who believe the schools do not concentrate enough on the basics apparently are highly verbal.

Parents are not as much in agreement about what the schools should concentrate on and how much emphasis should be given to the basics as critics of the schools believe. The parents who were surveyed believe that schools should provide children with help in areas other than subject-matter learning. They believe the schools should teach the basics *and* provide help with social and personal problems, moral development, vocational preparation, and other important things.

Parents' responses also show that they are not in agreement about what the schools should emphasize. A large proportion are poorly informed about possible alternative goals for schooling and what their children need or are doing. About the only thing parents really agree on is the time of the opening hour of school and the length of the school year. About 80 per cent say that both of these are about right.

Responses of Parents by Race and Economic Status —

William Green, one of my students, studied parents' perceptions of the schools as a function of the parents' races and their economic status, using data in the data bank [5]. Green selected schools in a large city system which could be classified as either predominantly white or black, and classified them as either high or low economic status. The criterion he used for determining economic status was the percentage of children in a school who received free lunches. A problem in his study was the fact that only a few of the schools could be classed as black with high economic status parents since the incomes of most of the black parents were low.

Green compared the responses of the parents in these four race and economic groups. He concluded that parents in the upper economic groups are generally more satisfied with their schools. Lower economic black parents are the least satisfied. They desire stricter discipline, stricter academic requirements, and more teacher help for their children on their homework. In contrast to such concrete goals, white parents value process-type goals which can help their children become more self-reliant. For example, they value good study habits and helping children learn how to solve their own problems.

Green found that upper economic white parents and lower economic black parents are comparable in their degrees of satisfaction with the job the schools are doing. In each group, about half are satisfied and half are dissatisfied. On the other hand, upper black parents strongly approve of the job the schools are doing while lower whites strongly disapprove.

Green's study adds further emphasis to the difficulties schools face in solving their problems. All parents do not think alike. Neither do their children.

Other Factors in Parents' Attitudes —

There are many factors which play a role in determining attitudes toward school. Research shows, for example, that the closer parents live to their children's schools, the more democratic school principals are described as being. People who live farther from their schools believe the principals are more autocratic. The difference probably results from the amount of contact parents have with school principals. The less contact parents have, the more the parents rely on the reports of children for forming their attitudes. Research also shows that the same kind of difference is present when the socio-economic status of parents is compared with their attitudes toward school. The richer the parents, the more autocratic the parents think school principals are. Psychological distance plays strange games.

References

1. See Feelings About School in R. E. Bills, *A System for Assessing Affectivity*. University: The University of Alabama Press, 1975.
2. Minder, C. A study of male and female factor structure on the FAS. Paper read at the Annual Meeting of the Mid-South Educational Research Association, Jackson, Mississippi, November 13, 1975.
3. Houston, C. E. The relationship between classroom decision-making processes and feelings about school. The University of Alabama, unpublished paper.
4. See Parent Inventory in R. E. Bills, *A System for Assessing Affectivity*. University: The University of Alabama Press, 1975.
5. Green, W. F. A study of racial and socio-economic differences in parental perceptions of their children's schools. Paper read at the Annual Meeting of the Mid-South Educational Research Association, Jackson, Mississippi, November 13, 1975.

Chapter Seven

School Practices:
Are the Schools Oppressive?

In the late 1960s and early 1970s the effectiveness of many of society's institutions was questioned, and schools became involved in the protests which gripped the nation. The education profession became concerned with what was happening, although it tended to remain on the defensive.

In this context the Association for Supervision and Curriculum Development approved a "study of oppressive practices in American schools [1]." A committee of 10 ASCD members was formed, and the basic objective of a study was framed in question form: "Are the schools oppressive?"

Educators from 450 representative school situations (according to geographic location, school size, holding power of the school, etc.) were invited to assist in collecting data relative to school practices. Students from one elementary school classroom, one junior high school classroom, and one senior high school classroom from 149 school districts across the country participated in the study. In all, 10,731 students were involved. Rating scale data were collected from the teachers and administrators who worked directly with each classroom group of students in the study.

Jack Frymier was responsible for organizing the study, providing leadership, selecting the sample of schools, making the school contacts, printing the instruments, distributing and collecting the instruments, and guiding the transfer of the data from answer sheets to computer tapes. I assisted in the design of the study, and helped Frymier formulate the rating scales and analyze and interpret the data. The data analysis was assisted by Catherine Bills Hawkins and Jill Frymier Russell. Most of the discussion which follows stems from analyses by Cathy and me.

It was assumed that opportunities to exercise personal choice are desirable and liberating, that is, nonoppressive. If schools are oppressive, choice is restricted. If schools are not oppressive, choice is expanded. Thus it was assumed that non-oppressive schools maximize opportunities for their students to control what is happening to them and to their futures.

Oppression is both a reality and a perception. A happy slave is oppressed even though the slave does not know it. People are oppressed whenever their choices are restricted even though they may not perceive that they are oppressed. Likewise, they are oppressed when they feel that their choices have been restricted and that other people are directing their futures.

The findings of the school practices study relating to school attitudes, decision-making, and relationship qualities are similar to those drawn from the data in the bank examined in previous chapters. The two sets of data reinforce each other.

The Passive Roles Expected of Students —

The school practices study shows that students view teaching and learning as an enterprise in which teachers and textbooks act upon them. Students believe that they are expected to assimilate passively facts and generalizations with little or no meaning for them. Students believe that teachers see them as clean slates to be written on.

Teachers and administrators admit that the content of the school curriculum comes from textbooks, not from experiences that have meaning in and for the lives of students. Students often find themselves studying things which have no meaning for them and which in this sense are irrelevant. Worse still, teachers and administrators view student discussion of controversial issues as being outside the realm of the schools' curricular system.

It is not surprising to discover that students view school as a place where: 1) they are not permitted to decide what they feel they need or are interested in studying, 2) they listen and respond and, presumedly, "learn," 3) they must proceed in their learning in "lock step" fashion, and 4) they cannot pursue to satiation the things in which they are interested and involved.

Contrast in Students', Teachers', and Principals' Perceptions —

Another interesting finding arises from comparing students', teachers', and principals' responses to the 25 items common to their rating scales. As shown by each of these common items, the further away one is from being directly influenced by school practices, the better things appear. In their responses, students, teachers, and administrators were asked to indicate on a four-point scale how often the school is "like this." The scale points were "Most of the time," "Often," "Not very often," and "Hardly ever or never."

Without exception, on each of the common items teachers said the school was characterized by the item more often than did students. And without exception, administrators saw the items as more characteristic of the school than did teachers. *Teachers and administrators believe that students have a greater voice in their own affairs than students do.*

Here are some of the 25 common items:

- On their tests, our teachers ask questions about important things.
- Students in this school are free to follow their own desires.
- Students are encouraged to think for themselves.
- I am not afraid to express my opinions here in this school.
- Students in this school can change things they don't like.

- Our teachers encourage us to talk about controversial things like religion and politics.
- Students are encouraged to criticize this school.
- The teachers in this school encourage open classroom discussion.
- In class we study those things which the students have said are important to them.
- The students in this school have a chance to write the rules and regulations.
- Everybody is treated equally by the teachers at this school.
- Everyone, no matter who, gets to have his say about things in our class.

Teachers and principals evidently believe that their schools *should* display characteristics such as the above. If they did not believe they were desirable, they would state that the items were not frequently characteristic of their schools. This is contrary to what they did.

The Student Rating Scales —

Items on the rating scales which students completed were grouped into six categories: Regulatory, Relationships with Students, Relationships with Teachers, Cognitive, Affective, and Physical. Items were assigned to each of the categories by use of the following definitions:

Regulatory. Policies and rules or actions which imply policies or rules even if not written down or verbalized.

Relationships. Items which involve perceived attitudes of teachers, other students, and so forth, or expressed attitudes toward any of these. Relationship items usually involve interaction of a student with someone else. (If the action comes from teachers, principals, parents, or other adults without interaction with the students, it is classed as Regulatory.)

Cognitive. Items dealing with the content of the curriculum, content of instruction, instructional methodologies or practices, goals of instruction, and so forth.

Affective. Items which involve the right to one's own opinions, feelings, or beliefs including those which directly show respect for students' rights to their own opinions or beliefs,

Physical. Items which pertain to the physical environment including the school plant, instructional materials, amount of lighting, and so forth.

Students responded to the survey items by giving two different types of ratings. The first of these, already referred to, is called the "How Often" responses. Students described how often their school was "like this" by checking one of four alternatives. Students also indicated their feelings about a practice on a "How I Feel" scale, again by checking one of four alternatives.

Oppression and Frequency of Practices —

The greatest amount of oppressive, as judged by the "How Often" responses, occurs in the Regulatory category. The second greatest amount occurs in the Cognitive category. And the third most oppressive category is the Affective category.

Students see the *least* oppressive aspect of their schools, as judged by their "How Often" responses, to be Relationships with their teachers. In conjunction with the "How I Feel" ratings, this says that oppressive practices by teachers are among the least frequently occurring of oppressive school practices and are felt less keenly by students than oppression in other areas. However, of the 45 items dealing with relationships with teachers, 80 per cent are felt to be oppressive. Although oppression by teachers is less than that from other sources, it is frequent.

Categories of Oppression —

The most oppressive aspect of the schools as shown by the analysis of the "How I Feel" responses are the Regulations with which students live. Two categories tie for second most oppressive. They are the Relationships with Students and

Affective categories. Students are bothered by these two areas and by Regulations more than any other aspect of school.

As judged by student ratings of items in which the "How I Feel" responses were less strong than the "How Often" responses, items in the categories of Regulatory, Cognitive, and Affective elicit less intense feelings than might be expected. Quite likely this is because of attitudes on the part of students that "That's what school is like." Students expect to be oppressed in these areas and are somewhat insulated against strong feelings.

Items in the categories of Relationships with students, Relationships with teachers, and Physical characteristics elicit much stronger feelings than would be expected on the basis of frequency of their occurrence. Students are very disturbed by their Relationship with students. The oppressive practices of other students hurt more than those from any other source.

The most oppressive student practices include older children picking on younger ones, students making fun of each other for what they believe, and being left out unless you are a member of a group or a gang. Oppressive practices of teachers include favoritism shown by some teachers for some students, the autocratic nature of teacher-student relationships, and the poor attitudes some teachers hold toward some students.

In the Cognitive category, the students are most oppressed by curricular and instructional demands that require them to learn a predefined body of subject-matter, and by having little opportunity to explore in meaningful ways the required subject-matter, let alone these topics which excite them such as religion and politics. Oppression in the Affective category stems from the same root as the Cognitive category. Students are not permitted to think for themselves, follow their own desires, nor criticize what is going on. Students believe their feelings are not as important to the teachers and the school as are the facts.

Oppression and Student Rebellion —

The oppression of schools as seen by the "How Often" responses stems from the widespread belief that education should stress the imparting of information from knowledgeable teachers to uninformed students. As a consequence, students' choices are reduced to a minimum, students' opinions are seen as having little worth, and teachers relate to students in autocratic ways. Students become frustrated, and repressive rules and regulations become necessary.

This latter finding is particularly important. During the student disturbances in the late 1960s and early 1970s, students rebelling against rules and regulations made them the center of controversy in many schools. As a result, schools formed committees of teachers, administrators, and students to formulate rules and regulations which students could accept. Most schools developed codes of conduct which were adopted by students for themselves — and, incidentally, for generations of students to come who would have no voice in formulating their own rules.

Our study of school practices shows that rules and regulations were not really the source of the oppression felt by students. They were only the symptom. The real problem was the nature of the school curriculum and of teaching practices. Because students resented the fact that their desires and interests were not important, they began to behave in unacceptable ways. Among other things, they dressed unacceptably, let their hair grow long, "cut" school, were tardy, and tried to burn the school down.

Schools did not understand the reasons for students' misbehavior and assumed it was the result of poor upbringing, alienation, a "generation gap," or something else. Thus they did not seek to change what they were doing; instead, they sought to change what the students were doing. They attempted this by regulating such things as hair and skirt lengths, beards, and other symptoms of students' rebellion. This increased the students' rebellion because they saw the rules as oppressive. So the rules and regulations became the center of the controversy whereas the real culprits, irrelevant curriculum content and autocratic teaching methods, remained unchanged.

Rules and Oppression —

Rules and regulations tend to be oppressive because they limit choice and freedom of movement. From the viewpoint of the students in the survey, school rules are too arbitrary, too numerous, and formulated by other people. Students resent the restrictive nature of school rules and regulations. The favoritism increasing from grade to grade is often the result of discrimination in the application of rules in the eyes of the students.

The study shows also that students see schools becoming more oppressive grade by grade until the compulsory attendance age is reached. This occurs even though there is a significant decrease in physical conflict among the students and in the use of physical force by one student against another. As students go up the grades, they seem to respect each other more. In high schools, oppression stems more from the impersonal nature of large schools and instructional methods than from conflicts among students.

Relationships with teachers show progressive deterioration with increase in grade. The psychological distance between students and teachers increases, apparently as a result of changing instructional patterns and emphases. Teachers become more distant and defensive, are less interested in students, listen less to students, and become more arbitrary in the eyes of students.

Depersonalization and Oppression —

The Cognitive category gives clues to the causes of the deteriorating relationships between students and teachers. As students progress through the grades, subject-matter emphases increase, there is an increasing concern for what is in textbooks, and there is less planning between teachers and students. There is less concern for the bigger issues in life and more concern for cognitive understandings and learnings. School becomes more routine. There is less opportunity for individuality and creativity, more attention to details and to seemingly unimportant details, and less classroom discussion.

The same pattern is shown by the Affective category. With increase in grade there is a corresponding decrease in teachers' interest in what students are thinking and feeling. Students see more insistence that teachers be followed without question, less opportunity to make decisions for themselves, stifling of creativity and initiative, less understanding of students, and less concern for students' personal problems. Most of these changes are the consequences of increased attention to the cognitive aspects of learning and to an increasingly rigid curriculum and increasingly rigid methods of instruction.

Sex and Race and Oppression —

School is more oppressive for boys than for girls. A double standard exists in the schools as judged by the responses of the boys and girls. Boys believe they are judged by a different and more rigid set of standards than girls. In Relationships with students, girls escape the brutal nature of the interpersonal relationships in which some of the boys are victimized by others.

School is more oppressive for nonwhite students than for white students. This oppression is seen as involving freedom of choice; quality of relationships with teachers; fairness in permitting students to present their side of a "story"; concern about dress, manners, and appearance; being punished without knowing the reasons for it; physical aggression of students against each other; blackmail; personal characteristics of teachers, and especially as these relate to teacher-student relationships; lack of certainty of teachers' feelings about students; favoritism; perceived differences in standards and rules; the amount of homework; teacher-made tests; lack of freedom of choice in what is to be studied, and how and when it is to be studied; and suppression of political activity. In each of these areas, white students report considerable oppression but less than that reported by nonwhites.

In contrast, items in the Cognitive category are more often oppressive for white than for nonwhite students. Some items in the Affective category depict the same condition. In these two categories, practices more oppressive for white than for non-white students include the textbook-centered nature of instruction, lack of freedom of choice in what is to be learned, lack of opportunities for students to alter the direction of instruction, absence of excitement in classroom discussions, paucity of concern for the larger issues in society, and others. In the Affective area, nonwhite students believe their teachers have more respect for their thoughts and that they are encouraged to think for themselves to a greater degree than reported by white students.

In Summary —

The oppressive nature of schools stems from current concepts of what an education should do for young people and of what effective instruction is. The current concept, as seen through the survey, is a communication process in which teachers tell students what they need to know in order to become knowledgeable. Several consequences result. Students' desires, feelings, and interests are ignored. Teachers adopt relationship roles with students which students find dissatisfying. As a result of students' frustration and attempts to reject such instruction, the schools adopt rules and regulations which become additional sources of oppression. As a result, schools oppress students.

The Findings in Perspective

The similarity of the conclusions from the Study of School Practices and from the data base which has been discussed are striking. The studies reinforce each other.

These data show that highly undesirable perceptions are held by students and their parents. The negative effects predicted earlier from the social, political, and economic climates are evident in the lives of students.

It is easy to conclude that these highly negative findings result primarily from school experiences. Such a conclusion is the theme of some critics for whom education is a favorite "whipping boy" for all of society's problems. It probably is true that schools are partially responsible for the negativity of the findings. There is no way of determining this from the data, however. Furthermore, placing exclusive blame on the schools for the negative findings means that important facets of the problem are being overlooked.

Schools are only one of the institutions that affect children. There are many others — the church, the family, and informal organizations. In addition, children are affected by their relationships with other children and with adults other than parents and teachers, by television, and by other factors. Of these influences, schools probably are one of the more important, but they may not be the most important, and they certainly are not the only important one.

The attitudes toward school, the perceptions of decision-making relationships, and the quality of interpersonal relationships with teachers reported by students tell at least as much about the homes, churches, and community environments of children and their society as they do about their school experiences. It is a distortion to place all of the blame for what is happening to young people today on the schools, overlooking the nature of the broader society in which they are functioning.

Schools are not the sole cause of the problems and the conditions described. But they cannot escape responsibility for doing what they can to prevent the further development of the problems and provide the most wholesome atmosphere possible to overcome them. Serious revisions of schools, their programs, and their teaching methods are necessary.

What direction should changes in schools take? Should they follow the "back to basics" movement currently being demanded by many parents and critics of education? The answer is "No." That movement calls for even less concern for self-concept, attitudes, and interpersonal relationships. It demands even more exclusive concentration on subject-matter learning than at present. The negative findings reported in this book are at least partially a result of the pressures schools have experienced since the mid-1950s to increase the emphasis on academics. They are the result, also of increased demands for accountability in the schools and abstract academic standards which ignore the interests, abilities, needs, and capacities of individual students. These pressures have contributed to the problems which have been described and have failed to solve the problems for which they were designed.

The task which faces the schools is enormous; no simplistic solution can suffice. Before a solution can be achieved, we must break through the current restricting and limiting concepts of what constitutes good teaching and reexamine the goals of education.

References

1. Frymier, J. R., Bills, R. E., Russell, J. Frymier, & Finch, C. Bills. A study of oppressive practices in schools. *Curriculum Theory Network*. Vol. IV, No. 4, 1975, 307-313.

Chapter Eight

Teachers' Role Concepts:

How They Work to Create or Inhibit Intelligence

Our society faces a crisis. The direction of development of our young people is unacceptable. Schools are unable to cope with the crisis, and, despite their best efforts, it continues to mount. What alternatives do the schools have to assist them in changing these trends? One alternative involves better ways of viewing teaching, learning, developmental goals for students, and methods of organizing schools and classrooms for instruction.

Instruction and Teaching

Although it is not obvious from the current public debate about teaching, the possible roles of teachers vary widely. The stereotyped lecturing role played by a teacher who is knowledgeable and communicates effectively is not the only possibility. Actually, this role is probably one of the least effective ones. As we have pointed out, a teacher cannot be effective without being knowledgeable, but effective teachers use their knowledge in many ways, and they seek widely divergent goals with students. This is an important point. To examine it more fully, we need to compare two opposing types of teaching.

People who believe the goal of schools should be mastery of the "basics" tend to view teachers as people who help students acquire large amounts of information. They believe that teachers do this best by lecturing, requiring large amounts of memorization, drill, and recitation. Many such people also believe that good teachers can subtly instill large amounts of knowledge into students without resistance even if what is being learned is not meaningful. The word which best describes this role is *instruction*. Textbook-centered instruction tends to treat all children in a classroom as if they were alike. That is, as if their aptitudes, capacities, abilities, motivations, interests, and so forth were identical with every other child. Further, people who endorse this type of teaching believe that all children could learn successfully if their teachers were capable and sufficiently demanding. They also believe that children could succeed in their classrooms if they really wanted to and that it is the job of teachers to make them want to.

There is a distinction between "instructing" and "educating." Instruction is a process in which an instructor attempts to provide information, understanding, and insight, and stimulates students to want to learn. It is a communication process in which a well informed person attempts to communicate understanding to another person or persons. It is aimed at limited objectives and attempts to help people be better informed or technically more proficient. Many people believe that this is all that learners need to become educated people. So they stress the importance of instructors being well informed, able to communicate their information effectively, and able to motivate students to want to learn.

Educating or teaching, though, seeks broader goals. Like instruction, the goals of teaching include knowledge, information, and technical proficiency. Teaching also includes broader purposes such as assisting learners to understand a process, learn how to analyze and synthesize, become thinking people, and become more creative. "Educating" is a process of "educing" or bringing forth concepts, meanings, and insights from people who have the necessary facts.

It is a view of teaching as "education" which led Carl R. Rogers to say:

It seems to me that anything that can be taught to another is relatively inconsequential, and has little or no significant influence on behavior . . . I have come to feel that the only learning which significantly influences behavior is self-discovered, self-appropriated learning [1].

Rogers does not say that anything that can be taught is inconsequential. He indicates that anything that can be taught by one person to another is *relatively* inconsequential in its effects on the learner's behavior. Since Rogers is concerned with behavioral change, he views such instruction as relatively unimportant since it has little effect on how people behave.

Kahlil Gibran also describes teaching as "education" in *The Prophet,* who responded to a plea to ". . . Speak to us of Teaching" by saying;

No man can reveal to you aught but that which already lies half asleep in the dawning of your knowledge. The teacher who walks in the shadow of the Temple, among his followers, gives not of his wisdom but rather of his faith and his lovingness. If he is indeed wise he does not bid you enter the house of his wisdom, but rather leads you to the threshold of your own mind [2].

Thus, effective teachers lead learners to the edge of their own awareness.

Exponents of "instruction" usually point out that it is the job of the schools to teach children "what they need to know." They ask, "How can children think if they don't have anything to think with?" This assumes that children live in a vacuum until they are taught something. A problem with instruction is that by the time children have learned what they "need" to know, all they can think is what they have been "taught" to think. Teaching, in the sense of education or educing, tries to provide a child with an open window on life; not a prepainted view.

Most people who discuss the merits of "instruction" make a number of assumptions. The most common is the belief that all children need to get the same things from school. A second is the belief that what children need at one time in their development is the same as they will need at another time. They believe, for example, that all children need to know how to read. No one disagrees with this. But are all children interested in learning to read the same things? Furthermore, once they learn to read, should they all *have* to read the same things at the same time? One child in therapy told me, "In school you read to learn how to read. I would rather read to learn something else."

In school, students need to be provided with specific information for specific purposes, for example, information that enables them to use English correctly. It does not follow, though, that they can be taught how to be creative in their use of English by teaching them the rules of English usage. Schools usually do this because it is assumed that at a later date students will be able to apply the rules creatively. However, there is much evidence to suggest that the reverse is true. Teaching rules makes students less able to write well. If schools help students use English creatively, they become more concerned with the mechanics and rules of writing which help them do this.

It is not valid to assume that all people at all times need only to be instructed. And it is certainly invalid to believe that they need only what they can learn by themselves without assistance. More likely, sometimes and in some subjects, people need to be given specific information; and at other times and in other subjects, they need more opportunities to learn by themselves. Students in vocational courses probably need a greater amount of instruction than students in liberal education courses. Teaching in the sense of educing lies somewhere between the extremes of forced learning and laissez-faire instruction.

Role Concepts of Teachers

I have made a series of six studies aimed at understanding more about how teaching can be conceptualized, and the relationships between these concepts and such things as teaching success, qualities of relationships with students, and students' perceptions of classroom decision-making. Some of these studies were made in universities and some in public schools.

The studies show that teaching role concepts do not differ significantly from each other at these two levels. The studies also support the belief that the undesirable situation described by the data base is at least partially related to teachers' role concepts.

Three of the studies of teaching role concepts were made in state universities, and extended over a period of 16 years from 1960 to 1976. These studies, made in three distinctly different state universities, gave highly similar results [3, 4]. There is a high degree of universality in the way people describe an ideal college level teacher. This universality extends across time, different institutions, different faculty members, and different students.

In each of the three studies, the data were subjected to a mathematical process called factor analysis. This process attempts to see if meaning can be found in large amounts of data. The descriptions in each of the three studies yielded five bipolar factors which were highly similar from study to study.

A bipolar factor is one which goes from an extreme point at one end of a continuum to an opposite extreme at the other end. The concept of hot-cold can be used to illustrate a bipolar continuum. One end would be extremely hot. Points closer to the middle would be less hot. As the mid-point is approached, temperatures become less and less hot; after it is passed, temperatures become cooler and cooler until the extreme cold point is reached.

The university studies led to the question, "Are the role concepts of public school teachers similar to those of college instructors?" To answer this question, role concept descriptions were collected from 550 public school teachers.

A factor analysis of these 550 role concept descriptions produced the same five bipolar factors as those which emerged from the university role concept studies. The five bipolar factors thus represent the common descriptions given ideal teaching roles as described from the primary grades through graduate school. Each of these four studies helped to clarify the meanings of the factors.

Factors in Teaching Roles

In the descriptions of the teaching role concept factors, the wordings of the items used in the instrument have been followed as nearly as possible so that the descriptions reflect the views of the people who sorted the statements. The five bipolar factors offer objective, research-derived means of describing the important dimensions of teaching as viewed by teachers and their students. The five factors are:

I. Opening or Focussing
II. Planning With or Planning For
III. Monitoring Students' Learning
IV. Responsibility for Learning
V. Guiding Student Learning

Opening or Focussing —

One end of Factor I deals with the pyramidal concept of education. This concept visualizes an educated person as having a broad base of general education or knowledge on which are built smaller and smaller increments of ever-increasing specialized knowledge and training. This end of the factor is called FOCUSSING. On this end of the factor, teachers focus students' attention on narrower and narrower educational goals until the students supposedly reach an educational pinnacle.

The opposite end of Factor I is called OPENING. On this end, teachers attempt to open their students to new experience and its personal meanings. Opening teachers seek to help students become more capable and self-reliant problem-solvers, while focussing teachers direct their efforts toward helping students learn what the teachers believe educated people need and ought to know. Whereas opening behavior aims at making students problem-solvers, focussing behavior aims at providing students with solutions to problems.

Teachers who idealize an opening role view teaching as an activity in which they seek to develop students' confidence in their own learning abilities. They treat each student as an individual with worth and integrity. They are sensitive to the meanings of students' behaviors as well as to their own. Such teachers free students for self-initiated learning by means of interactive, facilitating, and enabling relationships in which meaning and relevance are stressed. The goals of teaching are open-ended, and are determined by the students and the teachers in interaction. In general, these goals include helping students become independent learners by expressing and being responsible for their own ideas and through discovering information for themselves. Students' motivation to learn is internal and intrinsically related to the meaningful learning which is taking place.

The focussing end of the factor describes a role which is the converse of an opening role. Instructors see themselves as responsible for developing habits of scholarship in students through hard work and externally imposed standards. The goals of learning are determined by the instructors who assume authoritative teaching styles and attempt to motivate learners. Instructors strive to shape students' behavior according to the instructors' standards and purposes. Students' motivation is external and related to extrinsic rewards. Instructors use their superior knowledge and experience to make presumedly wise decisions for students. An important purpose of such instruction is to determine levels of students' scholarly competence.

Focussing instructors try to accomplish these goals by stressing factual learning and command of the subject, standardizing course requirements so that students can be objectively evaluated and compared, helping students stick to the facts in their thinking, seeing that knowledge and information are available through the use of good textbooks and lectures, and identifying for students what is important in the course. All students are seen as having the same academic needs, and what is important for one student to learn is believed to be important for all students.

Planning With or Planning For —

Factor II is called PLANNING. One end is concerned with planning *for* students; the opposite end is directed toward planning *with* students. In planning *for* students, teachers accept responsibility for making the final decisions. In planning *with* students, teachers work cooperatively with the students in arriving at decisions.

Instructors who plan *for* students assume responsibility for determining the framework and content of their courses. They organize their classes in terms of objectives which they define, outline the procedures to be used (including the nature of papers, term projects, and numbers and types of examinations), and help students achieve a comprehensive view of the topics being covered. They emphasize factual learning, and attempt to make their points clear by use of adequate examples and illustrations. They determine the goals of courses and tell students how they expect them to perform. They take responsibility for checking class attendance and for giving students grounding in the "basic" facts as they relate to the courses. They are purveyors of information.

Teachers who plan *with* students help students set their own course objectives and develop the framework within which their class will operate. In such classes there is an interactive student-teacher relationship in which the teacher works on a peer basis with students in an attempt to explore and understand reality. Such teachers lecture only when the class needs insights or information for which no other sources are available. These teachers attempt to release the creative leadership within the class group. They believe their teaching should reflect the attitude that students are motivated to improve and to change, when they are free to do so, in directions that have personal meaning and relevance for them.

Monitoring Students' Learning —

Factor III is called MONITORING LEARNING. Teachers who subscribe to one end of the factor monitor students' learning. Teachers at the opposite end help students learn how to monitor their own learning and to be responsible for it. They do this by helping students examine the personal meanings of what they are learning, become intellectually curious, explore beyond the limits of formal classwork, and develop questioning, analyzing, and synthesizing attitudes.

Some teachers adopt monitoring roles, however, in which they do such things as check class attendance, insure discipline and order, check students' progress, watch students carefully so they do not cheat, and persuade students to accept what is good for them. Teachers who assume responsibility for monitoring students' learning are, in effect, overseers. Conscientious teachers who seek such a role follow carefully defined classroom procedures in which they give frequent tests to assess students' progress and systematically check all assignments and written work. They feel that knowledge of results serves as reinforcement for effectively shaping desired student behavior. They carefully follow established policies.

On the other hand, teachers who attempt to help students monitor their own learning are concerned with both the cognitive and the affective aspects of their learning. They respect the rights of students to discuss controversial issues and raise relevant questions. Their primary objective is to select and effectively present information that has relevance and meaning for the learners so that motivation becomes internal, and the rewards of learning are intrinsic. They also provide viewpoints and information not contained in the textbook. They empathize with the feelings of students and with their ideas, and establish helping relationships with them in which they accept responsibility for monitoring their own learning.

Responsibility for Learning —

Factor IV is called RESPONSIBILITY FOR LEARNING and reflects opposed opinions about who is responsible for what is learned in the classroom. Is the responsibility the teacher's or the students'? Some teachers encourage students to be responsible for their own learning and help them to become increasingly responsible. Other teachers try to serve as pathfinders in the academic maze by making points clear through use of examples and illustrations, organizing materials so that the students find it easy to learn the required facts, anticipating problems, and making difficult topics easy to understand.

Teachers who try to help students assume responsibility for their own learning view teaching as a relationship in which they help the students to become self-directing. Their purpose is to enable students to become proficient learners by helping them develop questioning, analytical, and synthesizing attitudes.

Such teachers create atmospheres which help students to become intellectually curious and to find their own answers. These teachers strive to raise the "aspiration levels" of students by increasing their skills and by placing emphasis on long-range goals and values.

Teachers who assume that their role is to be responsible for students' learning often serve as the primary source for the learning. They attempt to teach students what educated people need to know by simplifying material in the textbook, anticipating learning problems, making it easy to learn the required facts, adjusting the pace of instruction to students' learning capacities, and providing study guides. These teachers often take a direct approach to teaching. They lecture so that students will know what is important, organize the main points to aid students' learning, and carefully outline the procedures which students are expected to follow in class. They assume responsibility for informing students about how they are being evaluated and where they stand at all times.

Guiding Students' Learning —

Factor V is called GUIDING LEARNING. This factor deals with the question, "Is the teacher responsible for guiding the learning of the students or for being sensitive to and receptive of the guidance and suggestions provided by students?"

Teachers who believe they are responsible *for* students' learning attempt to guide students to goals which the teachers believe desirable. Teachers who believe they should be responsible *to* students try to be sensitive to the feelings and suggestions of the students. They are dependable in agreements with students, open to students' suggestions about classroom management, and accept students' reactions as a source of professional growth.

Teachers who believe they are responsible *for* the students' learning see themselves as being responsible for stimulating the students' thinking and academic activities. They attempt to inspire and stimulate students to learn, give them a sense of appreciation for the significance of the subject, and increase their skills in thinking. These teachers try to instill in students a desire to learn. They act as academic salespersons.

Teachers who believe they are responsible *to* the students serve as resources for the students' learning. They serve as consultants to students, providing expert advice and furnishing bibliographies and other resource materials. To aid students, they are prompt and dependable in fulfilling their promises and commitments to them.

Parochial School Teachers' Role Concepts —

Norman Presse and I studied the role concepts of parochial school teachers to determine if their teaching role concept factors differ from those of public school teachers and college instructors [6]. We discovered that the *dimensions* of parochial school teachers' role concepts are almost identical to those of the other groups. We also found significant differences in the emphases given the five factors by the two groups of teachers. The ideal role concepts of the parochial school teachers, in comparison with public school teachers, show they are higher in planning *with* students, they plan less *for* students, and they see students as more responsible for their own learning.

These findings are interesting in view of a study of values of parochial and public junior high school students I made [7]. These students lived in a moderately large, mill city in the Northeast. Large numbers of people had moved to this city from Portugal to work in the mills and most of them were Roman Catholics. Almost 50 per cent of the city's children attend Catholic parochial schools.

When students in the public and parochial schools of the city were compared, important differences emerged. One of these concerns the values of the two groups. The parochial school students idealized traits such as responsible, sincere, honest, trustworthy, loyal, friendly, kind, obedient, reliable, and others much more than they are idealized by the public school students. These traits were measured by the self-concept instrument which was described earlier in this book.

The study also shows that the parochial school students, in comparison with the public school students, have greater feelings of inferiority, strive more for perfection, have more positive perceptions of other people, and are more highly motivated to succeed in school work. The public school students are more defensive and less amenable to change in their perceptions and motivation. The parochial school students are more often - + ("I am worth less than you are") whereas the public school students are more often + - ("I have greater worth than you do"). The parochial school students underrate themselves while the public school students overrate themselves.

These findings make it easier to understand the role concept differences reported by Presse and me [6]. It is easier to be open and to offer a facilitating role to young people who offer you little threat than to those who threaten you. Teachers' role concepts are influenced by the qualities of the students they teach.

Another study by David Nevin, a colleague, and me is also of interest in this context. Nevin and I reported the results of a study of "recently developed" private schools in the South [8]. One of the major conclusions of our study was that the inexperienced and poorly prepared teachers in these private schools offer more positive relationships to their students than do more highly qualified and experienced public school teachers in the same communities. The data show that the private school children are similar in values and attitudes toward themselves and other people to the parochial students described above and are significantly different from public school children in the same communities. The personal characteristics of public school children offer far more threat to public school teachers than the personal characteristics of the private school children offer their teachers.

Which Type is Best?

Repeated criticism of public education during the past two or three decades has produced a stereotype of an effective teacher. Many people have been led to believe that one end of each of the role concept factors represents a more desirable role than does the other. An effective teacher, according to this viewpoint, is one who focusses students' learning, plans for their learning, monitors their learning, is responsible for their learning, and sees the students as responsible to the teacher for their guidance. So deeply ingrained has the stereotype become in the minds of many people that it is difficult for them to believe that each of these concepts has an acceptable opposite.

But the data have shown that effective teaching is more similar to consulting. To be successful, consultants must help open clients to new alternatives or new ways of viewing their problems; they must help clients to plan; they usually help clients develop plans for evaluating their own efforts (monitoring); they help clients become less dependent and more fully accepting of their own uniqueness; and they are responsible *to* their clients, not *for* them. Effective teaching involves the same set of principles; teachers should serve as learning consultants for students.

References

1. Rogers, C. R. *On Becoming a Person.* Boston: Houghton-Mifflin, 1961, p 276.

2. Gibran, K. *The Prophet.* New York: Knopf, 1973, p 56.

3. Bills, R. E. *Improvement of Instruction through Teacher Description: A Presidential Venture Fund Project.* University: The University of Alabama, 1975.

4. Horton, C. S. *Faculty and Student Perceptions of Ideal Teaching Roles in a Small, State University.* The University of Alabama, unpublished doctoral dissertation, 1976.

5. Bills, R. E. Role concepts of public school teachers. *Proceedings: Mid-South Educational Research Association,* 6: November, 1977, p 75.

6. Presse, N. J. & Bills, R. E. A comparison of role concepts between public and parochial school teachers. *Proceedings: Mid-South Educational Research Association.* 7: November, 1978, p 118.

7. Bills, R. E. Perceptions of self and others of parochial and public school children. *Proceedings: Mid-South Educational Research Association.* 3: November, 1974, p 62.

8. Nevin, D. & Bills, R. E. *The Schools that Fear Built.* Washington: Acropolis Books Ltd., 1976.

Chapter Nine

The Teacher-Student Relationship

The Most Important Factor In Educating for Intelligence

The effectiveness of the roles teachers practice can be evaluated. The role concepts of teachers which emerged from the study of 550 teachers reported in the preceeding chapter provide one ingredient for such an evaluation [1]. Principals' ratings of the teachers' success and their areas of strengths and weaknesses are a second ingredient for the study. Additional available data for the evaluation include the race, sex, amount of teaching experience, and degrees of each teacher. The role concepts of the teachers were examined as functions of these variables.

Evaluating Teachers' Effectiveness —

Many people believe that the amount of knowledge a teacher has or how much students learn from a teacher can be used to measure teachers' effectiveness. Each of these has a weakness which invalidates its use for this purpose. For example, the use of teachers' knowledge as a measure of effectiveness assumes that teaching is an act in which a well informed teacher communicates knowledge to students. People who believe this also believe that the only effective teaching role is an instructional one. The assumption begs its own answer which may not be correct. If teaching is successful to the degree that teachers are well informed, it is also successful to the degree that teachers are capable of communicating this knowledge. Simply because a teacher is well informed does not assure that the teacher is also a good communicator.

Likewise, the amount which children learn during a school year is an equally ineffective criterion. Where instruction is departmentalized, it is impossible to determine which teachers are responsible for students' growth. Too, all students do not come to school equally well prepared to learn or equally desirous of learning. The reasons for these differences are many: experiential backgrounds, parental interest and expectations, adequacy of diet and rest, illness, physical handicaps, and others. Any of these can limit the educational progress of children even if they have effective teachers.

Three unpublished studies I made can be used to illustrate the problem teachers face in being effective with all children. In these studies, differences in students' achievement test scores from school to school within three school systems were studied. Both elementary and secondary schools were included although data were examined separately for each grade level. Each study involved a large number of schools, for example, the third city included 81 schools. The studies attempted to account for differences in achievement test results among the schools of a system.

The question for which an answer was sought was, "Are there factors which will help to explain why students in some schools achieve more highly than students in other schools in the same school system?" A variety of measures was used to predict achievement in the schools; measures of students' academic aptitudes, attitudes toward school, concepts of self and other people, the quality of decision-making and teacher-student relationships, parents' attitudes toward the schools, the percentage of black and white students in each school, and the number of students in each school who were certified to receive free lunches. This latter measure was used as an indicator of the economic status of the homes from which the students came.

Most of the variables studied were found to be related to the difference in achievement among the schools, but practically all of the difference could be accounted for by the economic status of the parents. In schools where many students were eligible for free lunches, achievement was low; in schools where only a few students were eligible, achievement was high. The average achievement in a school can be predicted more accurately from knowing the economic status of the students' parents than from knowing the students' academic aptitudes or a variety of other things.

Thus the effectiveness of teachers cannot be determined by measuring the achievement of their students any more reliably than the achievement of teachers can be used to measure their effectiveness. Because of this and other considerations, principals' ratings of teachers' success have been used in our studies of the effectiveness of the roles teachers practice.

Principals' Ratings and Teachers' Role Concepts —

In the role concept study, the 550 teachers were divided into groups according to the ratings of their success given them by their principals. The ideal role concepts of the groups were then compared. Teachers who idealize opening roles are rated as more successful by their principals than are their counterparts who idealize opposite characteristics.

More effective teachers idealize:	Less effective teachers idealize:
Opening students to experience	Focussing students' learning
Planning with students	Planning for students
Helping students monitor their own behavior	Monitoring students' behavior
Helping students become responsible	Being responsible for students
Being sensitive to students' suggestions	Guiding students

This conclusion supports an observation suggested by other studies. The role concept dimensions form two clusters. In one set, teachers idealize opening, planning *with*, student monitoring, student responsibility, and student guides. The other set of teachers idealize focussing, planning *for*, teacher monitoring, teacher responsibility, and teacher guidance. It is around these two differing sets of role concepts that much of the current argument about how teachers should teach revolves. The first of these roles will be referred to in the remainder of this book as "facilitating" and the second as "controlling."

The belief that teachers can be classed as "facilitating" or "controlling" must be qualified. If teachers were completely of one type or the other, they would not present serious problems for students. It is relatively easy to adjust to adults who are consistent in their behavior. Students might like one of the two types better but probably could learn from either. Unfortunately, many teachers are mixtures of both types, presenting inconsistent and difficult puzzles for learners to solve. A teacher may, for example, feel a desire to help young people learn how to think for themselves but try to do it by teaching them what to think. This type of teaching does not produce independent thinkers.

In the study of 550 teachers, principals rated teachers strengths and weaknesses in seven areas including: instructional content, discipline, relationships with students, work with other teachers, community involvement, work with parents, and extracurricular work. The study shows that principals see the teachers' greatest strengths concentrated primarily in four areas: instructional content, relationships with students, discipline, and work with other teachers. The data also show that the roles teachers idealize are not related to what principals perceive as the teachers' areas of strength. For example, facilitating teachers are not seen by their principals as stronger in instructional content or discipline than controlling teachers. Similarly, facilitating teachers are not seen by their principals as having more adequate relationships with students than controlling teachers.

Although the ratings of teachers' strengths are concentrated in four areas, ratings of teachers' weaknesses are spread throughout the seven areas of choice presented. According to principals, teachers can be strong in fewer ways than they can be weak. When the role concepts of the teachers were compared with their ratings of weakness, no relationships were found. Thus neither facilitating nor controlling ideal role concepts are associated with particular strengths or weaknesses. Neither facilitating nor controlling teachers are less strong in instructional content or discipline.

It is interesting that instructional content is seen as the area of teachers' greatest strength but only infrequently as the teachers' area of greatest weakness. All the teachers in the study are duly certified and have at least the minimum amount of training in instructional content necessary for the positions they hold.

Role Concepts and School Level —

The role concepts of the elementary and secondary teachers in the group of 550 teachers were compared. This comparison resulted in the firmest conclusion of the study. *Elementary and secondary teachers perceive their roles in significantly different ways.* Elementary teachers idealize facilitating roles, while secondary teachers and those teaching in departmentalized schools seek controlling roles. As we go up the scale of school grades, the role concepts of teachers change from facilitating to controlling.

Sometimes this change is abrupt, such as between elementary schools with self-contained classrooms and departmentalized middle schools. The same abrupt change is found between elementary schools and junior high schools, and between elementary schools with eight grades and high schools.

These changes in role concepts from grade to grade parallel the negative changes in students' feelings about themselves and other people, the types of decision-making in their classrooms, the quality of interpersonal relationships between teachers and students, and the attitude of parents toward the schools.

Teachers see their job differently in upper grades than in lower grades. The parallel changes in students and their parents suggest that the changes in role concepts may cause some of the negative changes in students and their parents.

The changes in idealized role concepts with change in school grade reflect teachers' beliefs about how they must teach to be effective. Many teachers believe that effective teaching of subject-matter must be teacher-directed. There is nothing, however, which ties intellectual activity to textbook-centered instruction. Nor does study in any subject-matter area require that teachers assume responsibility for students and their learning.

Role Concepts and Other Teacher Characteristics —

The strongest relationships between ideal role concepts and variables such as age, teaching experience, sex, and race are with teachers' sex and race. Men and women and black and white teachers hold significantly different teaching role concepts. White women teachers differ significantly from white men teachers. White women teachers idealize facilitating roles more than white men do; white men idealize controlling roles more than white women teachers do. The "macho" role stereotype is evident. An interesting exception is that there are no significant differences between the ideal role concepts of black men and black women teachers.

The greatest differences in the four race-sex groups of teachers are those between black and white teachers. Black teachers idealize controlling roles to a greater degree than white teachers; white teachers idealize facilitating roles to a greater degree than black teachers. Differences in the experiential backgrounds of black and white teachers are probably important determiners of the difference in their ideal role concepts.

Role Concepts and Teacher-Student Relationships

A series of studies made by some of my students and me is relevant to this discussion of correlates of teaching role concepts [2, 3, 4]. In combination with other studies reported in this chapter, the studies show that in all grades, teachers who idealize facilitating role concepts are described as more interactive and student-centered and less teacher-centered than those who idealize controlling role concepts. Facilitating teachers are also described as having high levels of positive regard for students, being more empathically understanding, being less conditional in their expression of their regard, and being more honest in their relationships with students.

Relationships between idealized teaching roles, teachers' races and sexes, and students' races and sexes are complex, but teachers who idealize facilitating roles are seen by students in a more positive light than are teachers who idealize controlling roles.

The different role concepts idealized by men and women teachers and by black and white teachers, in combination with differences in the ways black and white and female and male students perceive their teachers, is of extreme importance. A mixture of teachers by race and sex presents difficult adjustment problems for girls and boys and for black and white children. The adjustments required of students in a typical school probably exacerbate learning, personality, and relationship problems for many children. These are variables which must be considered in school organization, design of curricula, and instructional methods.

Teaching Success and Teacher Characteristics

The educational research literature includes many studies which have attempted to relate teaching success to teacher characteristics. This research has added little to our understanding of what is required for teaching success. It adds even less about the nature of teaching.

One of the major thrusts of my work in this area has been an effort to determine the qualities of teachers which are associated with their teaching styles and their reception by students. My interest was prompted by the work of psychologist Carl R. Rogers, who proposed that a significant difference in people is in the extent to which they are open to the meanings of their experience. By this he meant all experience has individual personal meaning. People who are open to these meanings respond in ways consistent with them. Others respond in ways which conflict with their personal meanings. Such inconsistencies lead to personal discomfort and maladjustment.

Openness to Experience —

Rogers holds that psychological "sickness" occurs when people are not open to their experience and its personal meanings for them. Such people often do not have the data of their experience available to them because they blank it out of their minds. When it is available, its meanings are frequently distorted. Because of this, their behavior is usually based on incomplete information, defensive, inappropriate, and unimaginative.

People who are closed to their experience offer other people poor interpersonal relationships. The more open people are to their experience, the less stereotyped is their behavior and the more personally rewarding it is. In addition, open people — being less threatening — can provide relationships to assist other people in becoming more open. In a climate of reduced threat, it is less necessary for people to be defensive and to deny and distort experience and its meanings. They become more open to experience and change their behavior correspondingly.

As described earlier, helping relationships are characterized by high levels of unconditional positive regard, empathic understanding, and congruence. These are the characteristics we examined to determine the qualities of students' relationships with their teachers.

Rogers studied openness by using recorded interviews of psychotherapy interviews. From these studies, he described the characteristics of people which can be used to judge their degrees of openness to experience.

Teacher Openness and Teacher Problems —

In the 1950s, I became interested in the problems of teachers and in what these tell us about teachers' openness to experience. It was my belief, later confirmed by research data, that open teachers are more successful in their teaching than are less open teachers. Because of this, I collected problems of teachers and used a sample of these to enable teachers to describe their most pressing problems. I then factor-analyzed the descriptions of 2,635 teachers to see if their descriptions could be used to measure their degrees of openness to experience.

The analysis showed that teachers' problems could be used to measure their openness. I also confirmed the fact that teachers could be described along a continuum of openness to experience in terms suggested by Rogers' earlier work.

Teachers' problems are concerned, primarily, with the ways they deal with new experience or their need to defend themselves against the meanings of old experience. Their problems contain an *attitudinal dimension* which can be described as positive-negative. The more positive the attitudes reflected in the problems, the more open a teacher is to experience. Conversely, the more negative the attitudes, the more defensive and less open is the teacher.

A second dimension is concerned with the *locus of responsibility* for doing something about the problem. The more responsibility is accepted by the teacher, the more open is the teacher. If a teacher sees students as responsible for solving the problems, the teacher is less open to experience. Another way of stating this is to ask, "Who must change if the problem is to be solved: the teacher or the student?"

Another dimension is the importance of the problem. The more open the teacher, the more likely the problem is a significant or *central* one. Less open teachers are more concerned with *peripheral* problems or with problems of lesser importance. Being concered with a peripheral problem keeps people from looking at more central ones. It enables them to defend themselves.

The *time dimension* is also important. Open teachers see the solutions to their problems as somewhere in the future. They may be interested in the past but only as it helps them to understand the present and predict the future. Less open teachers look to the *past* for solutions to their problems. Their feeling is, "If things were only like they used to be —." They long for the "good old days."

The problems of teachers can be used to illustrate these dimensions. One of the problems in the sample says, "My most pressing problem is teaching children who lack the desire to learn." This problem implies a negative attitude toward the children (they do not desire to learn). The locus of responsibility for the solution to the problem is within the children; the children, not the teacher, will have to change before the problem can be solved. The time orientation of the problem is the present. It is concerned with what the children are like now. The problem is also a peripheral one. If the problem were expressed as, "My most pressing problem is the fact that the children are not learning as I think they should," it would reflect a more central problem and a greater degree of openness.

An example of a more open problem is the statement, "My most pressing problem is learning new ways of helping students develop their maximum potentials through school work." The implied attitude toward children is positive. They are worth the effort required to help them. The locus of responsibility for the solution of the problem is in the teacher since the teacher must change in order to solve the problem. The problem is a central one, and it looks to the future for its solution.

The importance of this analysis of teachers' problems becomes apparent when several studies are reviewed. The study by Emmerling discussed earlier (page 80) shows that teachers' interpersonal relationship qualities as described by their students are products of the openness of the teachers. The more open the teachers, the more they provide helpful relationships characterized by a high level of positive and unconditional regard, empathic understanding, and congruence.

The study by James Finch also referred to earlier (page 25), shows that college instructors who are more open to their experience are seen by their students as having a better quality of relationships with them than instructors who are less open to their experience.

In a study of a large city school system, I asked teachers to describe their most pressing problems. The principals of these teachers then rated the teachers' success. The problems' descriptions were scored for openness, and these scores were compared to the teachers' success ratings. The results show that the more open the teacher, the more successful the teacher is judged to be. So more open teachers provide more helpful relationships for students and are viewed as more successful.

Openness of Elementary and Secondary Teachers —

In this large city school system, I compared the openness of the elementary teachers with the openness of the high school teachers. (The system had eight-year elementary schools and four-year high schools.) The elementary teachers were much more open than the high school teachers.

The difference in the openness of the two sets of teachers can be seen by comparing the descriptions given by the two groups. Elementary teachers rated the following illustrative problems as more pressing:

- Finding time to do needed individual work with pupils
- Learning new ways of reaching the slow and fast learner
- How, in spite of the many handicaps that face me, can I be the best possible teacher I can be
- Learning new ways of helping children develop their maximal potentials through school work
- Changing teaching practices to fit the needs of individual students
- How to continue to improve my teaching in a fast changing world
- Learning better ways of evaluating pupil progress.

In contrast, the high school teachers listed problems such as the following as their most pressing ones:

- Students' lack of knowledge of the fundamentals
- Getting children to put forth the necessary efforts to accomplish the task assigned
- Inability on the part of children to think for themselves
- Lack of interest shown by students
- Motivating children to want to do more than just pass
- Inability of some students to have a spark of ambition.

The items in these two groups show important differences between the groups. Elementary teachers express concern for the children and for their learning. Instructional problems arise from individualizing instruction and helping individual children learn.

The high school teachers' problems are concerned mainly with students' characteristics. They believe that students lack knowledge of the fundamentals, do not use their time wisely, are lazy, are unable to think for themselves, lack interest, do not want to develop high standards, are easily satisfied with merely passing grades, and lack ambition. With students like these, the teachers reason, how can they expect to be successful? The value of these problems in defending teachers against feelings of failure is easy to see.

A major difference in the two groups of teachers can be gleaned by reading between the lines. Elementary teachers, expecting children to differ from each other, know they must individualize instruction. High school teachers, on the other hand, believe that they cannot teach adequately because of what the students are like, due partly at least to students' inadequate preparation. High school teachers believe that their job is to teach the same things to all students and that the teaching should center around subject-matter. *Elementary teachers are interested in teaching children; high school teachers are interested in teaching subject-matter.*

Another former student, Harry Engle, tested the thesis that more open teachers can profit more from an opportunity to learn than can less open teachers [5]. Engle tested experienced teachers at the beginning and at the end of a summer workshop designed to help them develop plans for attacking their students' learning problems. He discovered that although the less open teachers in the workshop showed no significant change, the more open teachers changed significantly and developed even more positive and accepting attitudes toward themselves and toward other people than they had at the beginning of the workshop.

Openness and Threat —

Charles Minder, another student with whom I worked, studied teacher openness as a function of the races of teachers and their students [6]. He found that black elementary teachers are more closed to their experience than are white elementary teachers regardless of the predominant student race of the school in which they teach. This difference was not found at the high school level. It would have been difficult to find a difference at this level because neither black nor white high school teachers are an open group of teachers.

Minder also found evidence to support his belief that the openness of black and white teachers in predominantly black schools is not significantly different from that of black and white teachers in predominantly white schools. Differences among schools are so great that they cancel out differences between the races.

Minder's most important finding was in regard to the effects of the races of the students and teachers on the openness of the teachers. He found no significant difference in his elementary schools. At the high school level, though, he found that black teachers who teach in predominantly white schools are less open to experience than black teachers who teach in predominantly black schools; and that white teachers who teach in predominantly black schools are less open than white teachers who teach in predominantly white schools. It may be that teachers who "cross over" are less open to experience than their counterparts. It is more likely that since threat to teachers is greater in high schools than in elementary schools, students are seen to pose far greater threats for teachers of the other race than for teachers of the same race.

There is an encouraging note in Minder's findings. When the interaction of the teachers' and students' races are examined across schools, it is clear that the threat students pose for teachers of the other race is not the same from school to school. In some schools it is greater, and in some it is reduced. Minder believes this is probably due to the principals' leadership. Principals can, through leadership, negate the threats experienced by black or white teachers in a school where the predominant student race is different from theirs. Would effective leadership help high school teachers become as open as elementary teachers? It is doubtful. Quite likely, elementary teachers teach at that level because of their interest in children and high school teachers teach there because of their interest in subject-matter.

Students' Suggestions for Improving Schools

Students' opinions can be useful in understanding successful teaching and the roles teachers should play. I once asked a group of sixth graders about their likes and dislikes in teachers. These are some of their likes:

- Cheerful smile and nice clothes
- Thoughtful
- Understanding
- Believing what you say
- Letting you explain something
- A little sense of humor
- A teacher who does not expect complete perfectness
- Teachers who help students individually if they need it
- Teachers who explain things in detail and go over things twice if students need it
- Teachers who don't like special people in their room
- Teachers who are kind when you're nice.

Here are some of their dislikes:

- Teachers who don't listen to students opinions and thinks he's always right
- Teachers that are never funny, just always serious
- Teachers who give too much homework and not just enough to let you learn something
- Teachers who go around telling one thing and doing another
- Teachers who make class boring
- Teachers who teach us what we should know the next year
- Teachers who accuse someone wrongly
- Teachers who breathes (sic) down your neck and watch everything you do

- Teachers who get mad at you if you are not late for class but everyone else is in the room
- Teachers who ask someone to take names when she goes out of the room because that shows that she does not trust the class
- Teachers who have favorites in the room and let them do everything
- Teachers who don't listen to you.

I worked with a school faculty in its effort to improve their school. We started by collecting information about how the students felt about the school. After the responses were scored and tabulated, the teachers took the tabulations back to their rooms and asked the students if the results really showed what the school was like. They then asked the students to give suggestions for improving the school. The teachers shared the results with each other and agreed on a set of generalizations about what the students said. Some of these are:

- The students would like for teachers to know them better as people.
- Teachers should apply rules equally. They treat their "pets" differently.
- Teachers should communicate greater personal interest in the students.
- Teachers might have personal conferences with students to apprise them of their progress, problems, and deficiencies.
- The students would like a better opportunity to talk with the teachers so that they can tell them what they are thinking and feeling.
- Students desire more opportunity to participate in their evaluation.
- Students are bored. To relieve the boredom, they want teachers to ask them for their opinions and to give them opportunities to suggest alternatives.
- Teachers talk too much and say too many unimportant things.

- Teachers think more highly of children who are neat, who do well in sports, who have more academic ability, who are cleaner, and who have better personal appearances.
- The students want to be treated more as adults; to have their opinions considered more, to be consulted more often, and so forth.
- Teachers do not protect the rights of students. They desire a fair trial. They want all sides to be heard.
- The students would like to know the teachers better in a more personal manner.
- When the teachers are bored, the students would like to know how to help. When a teacher feels badly, they would like to know and to be able to help.
- Teachers frequently embarrass students. One source is the failure of teachers to protect confidential information including records and things told in confidence.
- Students desire to have their opinions more highly regarded. Differences of opinion should be allowed even if these disagree with the text.
- Students desire to be treated as individuals. Too frequently there are generalizations such as, "You people are all alike."
- Teachers should be more careful in how they say things to avoid "cutting" the students.
- Embarrassment should be eliminated as a means of controlling students; bringing a student back into a group; motivating a student to pay attention; motivating students to do better, and so forth. Such embarrassment usually stems from the use of sarcasm on the part of the teacher.
- There is insufficient two-way communication.
- Students want to be involved in the planning of units of work.
- Students want teachers to know them better as individual people and to evaluate them less as people.
- Students feel powerless at times to change some things they believe are important to change.

Two things stand out in the students' comments: 1) they are concerned about the quality of the relationships which exist between them and their teachers; 2) they are concerned about their lack of opportunity to affect decisions which are made in their classrooms.

In regard to interpersonal relationships between teachers and students, the students want their teachers to regard them as important people, to try to understand them, to be less conditional in their regard for them, and to be more honest with them. In regard to decision-making, students want opportunities to enter into these and to be able to affect their futures. They especially want to be heard so that their feelings will alter what is done in their classrooms.

What students are saying is that they want their teachers to hold facilitating role concepts. Such roles would help them to become more open to their own experience and its personal meanings. In these roles, teachers would plan more with them, would help them monitor their own learning, and would help them to become more responsible for their own learning. Such a role would show students that teachers are responsive to their suggestions and feelings.

Effective Teaching Roles

What the children in the above schools say is also what the cited research says. Teachers have a choice of teaching roles. One role is a facilitating one. The other — the obverse — is a controlling one. The freeing role is associated with the more successful teachers. The controlling role more often seen in less successful teachers though, is the role which many critics of public education believe teachers should adopt. It is the critics' contention that teachers can teach in this role *and* make children like it. If the students do not like it, there is something wrong with the teacher.

If we listen to students, we hear them say that teachers have already adopted a controlling role. This role is rejected by students, and their rejection is important. *No one can teach anyone anything they do not want to learn.* It is possible to make students give an appearance of compliance, but underneath hostility and rejection develop. In such conditions students do not find personal meaning in what they have "learned" and they are unable to apply it when they have need for it. Students forget what they have "learned" in class unless what they have learned has personal meaning for them.

Probably the most important of the research findings is the series of studies which show important relationships among teaching role concepts, classroom decision-making, perceived relationships with teachers, students' feelings about themselves, other people, and their schools, and parents' attitudes toward the schools. The most important component in these interrelationships is the teacher's role concept.

References

1. Bills, R. E. Role concepts of public school teachers. *Proceedings: Mid-South Educational Research Association.* 6: November, 1977, p 75.
2. Presse, N. J. *Students' Perceptions of the Decision-Making Process and Quality of Relations with Teachers as a Function of Race.* The University of Alabama, unpublished doctoral dissertation, 1977.
3. Phillips, D. J. *Teachers' Role Concepts and the Qualities of Teacher-Student Relationships.* The University of Alabama, unpublished doctoral dissertation, 1978.
4 Bills, R. E. & Griffin, E. W. Relationships of students' sex and race, teachers' sex and race, and teachers' role concepts to students' perceptions of teachers' decision-making and interpersonal relationship qualities. *Proceedings: Mid-South Educational Research Association.* 8: November, 1979, p 62-63.
5. Engle, H. A. *A Study of Openness As a Factor in Change.* Auburn University, unpublished doctoral dissertation, 1961.
6. Minder, C. *Teacher Openness As a Function of Race.* The University of Alabama, unpublished doctoral dissertation, 1976.

Part III

Drawing Up A Blueprint For The Creation of Intelligence

Chapter Ten

The Big Issues:
Freedom Vs. Control And Innate Vs. Learned Intelligence

Each of the two major types of ideal teaching role concepts, controlling and facilitating, in its own way, affects the relationships of teachers and students and decision-making. The roles also affect how students feel about their schools, how they see themselves and other people, and how their parents view the schools. The success of teachers is directly related to the teaching roles they idealize.

The roles are also the center of a continuing controversy. Adherents to the controlling role believe that quality can be achieved in elementary and secondary education only if the schools demand more serious efforts from students. They believe teachers and schools must concentrate more on "the basics" if students are to be educated adequately. People who believe that the proper role of the schools is to teach students what they need to know also believe that if students are not taught discipline and responsibility, they will not achieve them. They believe that students must undergo an apprenticeship in being responsible before they can act responsibly. They also believe that people cannot think unless they have something to think with, and that it is the job of the schools to provide the basic facts which they can use to think with.

Adherents of the facilitating role concept also believe that students need to have command of the basics. But they believe that students cannot become responsible adults simply because they are well informed. They believe that young people need opportunities to exercise responsibility for themselves if they are to develop as mature, responsible adults. They reject the notion that being responsible to adults develops the ability to be responsible for oneself. They contend that responsible, thinking, and sensitive adults develop from young people who have had many opportunities to think for themselves, be responsible for themselves, and interact extensively with other people.

Contradictions such as those represented by these two teaching role concepts are not unique to teaching. Many parents believe that if you want a child to grow up to be a responsible person, you should "bend the twig" the way you want it to grow. They believe that when the twig has been bent sufficiently, the child has no option other than to act responsibly. Other parents ask, "Does 'twig bending' produce responsible behavior on the part of children? And will behavior which is seen as responsible today continue to be seen that way in the future?"

Free-Will or Determinism?

The confusion is not limited to schools and teaching. It is an extension of the arguments regarding the nature of man and parallels questions that have bothered people for a long time. One of these asks, "Are our destinies determined for us or are we free to choose them?" The debate has its origin in theology but it permeates our thinking and leads to unresolved and perhaps unresolvable conflicts in people's beliefs.

Psychology, like education, has not escaped the controversy or its consequences. Some of psychology's most heated arguments during the past 35 or 40 years have involved adherents of one or the other of these points of view. Since education is based in part on psychology, it has shared psychology's dilemma.

Freedom or Control —

The argument within psychology was given a platform in 1976 when the American Psychological Association built its annual meeting around the theme, "Prospects for Control and Implications for Freedom." [1] Several of America's most outstanding psychologists were invited to share their thoughts on the theme. Two of the participants were B. F. Skinner and Carl R. Rogers. It was not unexpected that these two giants of American psychology would be invited to participate since 20 years earlier at another meeting of the American Psychological Association they had addressed themselves to "Some Issues Concerning the Control of Human Behavior." [2] Their 1956 positions remained essentially unchanged in 1976.

Skinner began his remarks by stating that:

To govern once meant simply to guide but the word soon acquired stronger meaning. Governments compel obedience to authority. In other words, they treat people aversively; punishing them when they behave badly or relaxing the threat of punishment when they behave well. . . . But why should governments confine themselves to aversive control? Rather than punish behaving badly, why not positively reinforce behaving well?

Rogers built his contribution around this statement:

The greatest amount of creative power is released not when individual behavior is controlled but when choice and power are consciously owned and utilized by the individual not taken from him or her.

Here in a nutshell are two opposed philosophical positions regarding the nature of people and what it takes to help them operate constructively and perhaps creatively. These are the same philosophical positions which emerged from the studies of teachers' ideal role concepts which we labeled "controlling" and "facilitating."

Operant Conditioning —

Skinner describes his work as *operant conditioning*, which means the conditioning of behaviors that organisms use to operate on their environments. To Skinner, there is no argument about the nature of mankind; there is only a reality. People behave as they do because their behavior has been shaped and conditioned by their environments. According to him, we are products of our past reinforcements. We behave as we do because of the reinforcements we receive for behaving this way. If the reinforcements are withdrawn, we will quit behaving as we did. We will then begin to behave in different ways if we are reinforced for doing so.

Both Skinner and his students have demonstrated that they can get organisms to respond as they desire by controlling the reinforcements the organisms receive. Being reinforced is made contingent upon behaving as the experimenter (teacher) desires. For example, suppose you desire to condition a rat to press a bar on a signal. You can do this by reinforcing any behavior of the rat which is involved in pressing the bar. The first step is to make the rat hungry so it is motivated. Then you begin to reinforce the rat by giving it a pellet of food if it looks at the bar. If it takes a step toward the bar, it gets another pellet. If it touches the bar, it is again reinforced. Very shortly, the rat is doing little else except pressing the bar and receiving reinforcement — until satiated by food. If you want the rat to continue, you must make certain that it continues to be motivated by hunger or thirst or by some other sufficiently strong motive.

Once the rat is conditioned to press the bar, it is possible to create complex patterns of bar-pressing behavior such as pressing the bar when a green light is shining and not pressing it for a red one. Or the rat can be conditioned to press the bar at certain time intervals and then wait a period of time before pressing it again. Such behaviors are produced by giving reinforcement only when the experimenter desires that the rat press the bar.

The effectiveness of Skinner's means of controlling behavior has been demonstrated in the training of many kinds of animals for a variety of purposes. Most obedience schools for dogs use the principles. Dancing chickens, seen sometimes at carnivals, have been "taught" to mount a phonograph record or other disk and "dance" for the reinforcement they will receive. Trainers reward their animals after acceptable performances.

There is nothing mysterious about Skinner's findings. We all know that people will do a lot of things for money or for other rewards. From Skinner's work we know that rats and pigeons will also work for rewards *if they want them* and once they know what must be done to obtain them.

There are many things which must be considered before adopting reinforcement theory as a basis for teaching students. For example, the application of operant conditioning to classrooms presents a serious problem. It uses deficiency motivation. Teachers cannot motivate children by withholding food or water. Skinner believes this is not a problem, though, and that reinforcement provided through knowledge of results is a sufficiently strong motivation to cause children to learn in school by operant conditioning. It is doubtful that knowledge of results can be as reinforcing for most students as food is to a hungry animal. Furthermore some students feel punished instead of rewarded by getting correct results under some circumstances, as when they are trying to attract attention.

If rewards are discontinued, there is no assurance that the behavior we are "paying" for will continue. Even though children may retain what they learned while being reinforced, they cannot be expected to continue to do things such as study schoollike subjects after they leave school if all they have been working for are the reinforcements. Perhaps this is why so few people continue to pursue their learning after they leave school — they were working either for the rewards of good or passing grades, for approval, or to avoid the punishment of failure. If so, they were not internally motivated.

It has also been found that rewarding behavior that starts out intrinsically satisfying may stop the behavior if the rewards are first made extrinsic and then discontinued. The psychological literature tells about a child who liked to practice the piano. Because the child was so diligent, the parents decided to reward her with money for each practice session. At a later date, when the reward was discontinued, she found piano practice no longer satisfying.

Operant conditioning has other weaknesses as an instructional methodology but it also has advantages. For example, it may be used to teach basic skills, and it probably should be used for this purpose when students are not intrinsically motivated. Students must have these skills just to cope with life.

Skinner believes that his emphasis has been on how organisms learn. This is debatable. His concern has been with teaching, not learning. He has learned, for example, much more about what he must do to get an animal to respond as he desires than about what happens to the animal during the process. Learning is assumed to have occurred when an animal which formerly would not press a bar now does so to receive food.

A more appropriate description of what has happened is that Skinner has learned how to communicate to an animal what it must do if it wants to be fed. Even the use of the term "reinforcement" may be misleading. Reinforcement can be defined only in terms of its effects. If the behavior Skinner desires increases following the use of a "reinforcer," the reinforcement is said to be reinforcing. The organism plays an important part in this definition. It will perform only if it wants food. There is nothing magical about food that makes it reinforcing. In fact, food is not reinforcing to a well-fed rat. Recently behaviorists have modified Skinner's position to include the organisms's view of its experience in their explanations of behavior and their understanding of reinforcement. Behavior control, however, still remains their purpose.

Skinner and his students have attempted to use reinforcement as a means of "teaching" in schools. Applications have included such things as programmed textbooks, teaching machines, and computer-assisted instruction. Although many devices using reinforcement theory have been enthusiastically introduced, most have failed to fulfill the claims of their proponents. The problem of motivation is probably basic to these failures.

Freedom to Be —

Skinner continues to elaborate on his ideas and has recommended them as the basis for systems of government. Such use was advocated in his *Walden II* and *Beyond Freedom and Dignity*. The quotation cited earlier in this chapter (page 147) was made in the context of what government should attempt to do with people.

Skinner believes that the purpose of government is to control people — for their own good, of course. He holds that governments treat people aversively and punish them when they behave badly. He believes this is a misuse of reinforcement theory. Instead of punishing people for behaving badly, governments should reward them for behaving well. To Skinner these are two sides of the same coin. But are they?

When a government such as ours punishes people for behaving badly, it is because those who are doing the punishing are attempting to erase a particular behavior, or to minimize it, or to limit its appearance and protect the right of other people to be secure from such behavior. When our society punishes certain behavior, it does not set limits on other behavior which is not unapproved. Our society does not attempt to say what we can do. It is concerned only that certain specific things not be done. In our society, people who are not engaged in unacceptable behavior are free to behave anyway they desire.

If we were to begin to reward people for "behaving well," we would need to develop a list of approved behaviors. People who were doing things on the approved list would be reinforced and those engaged in other behaviors would not be reinforced. According to reinforcement theory, the unapproved, unrewarded behavior would disappear and people would begin to behave in approved ways for which they were rewarded. But is this what we mean by freedom and democracy? Is not being permitted to behave in certain specific ways the obverse of being made to behave in approved ways? One choice says you cannot do certain things, while the other choice says you can do only certain things.

Roger's position, a direct contrast to Skinner's, represents the other horn of the educational dilemma. Rogers believes that what people do should be consistent with the meanings of their experience, that is, the personal meanings they assign things. He argues that we should free people to "become" their experience. What this means is that people's personalities are formed by their experiences to such an extent that we can say they "are" their experiences; and that we should encourage people to interpret their own experiences in terms of its personal meanings for them. Thus people should be open to their own experience and its personal meanings and their behavior should be consistent with these meanings.

His position is not that people are basically good but that they can respond only to their own meanings, that they have no choice but to do this. He does believe that the behavior of people who are open to their experience and its meanings is trustworthy. Such people know what it means to be hurt, deprived, lonesome, and depressed. They also know what it means to be fulfilled. They choose to assume control over their destinies; and in so doing, they are sensitive to other people. Open people utilize as much of their experience as possible in deciding what to do. They consider its implications for themselves and for other people.

Rogers received the gold medal award from the American Psychological Foundation for his contributions to scientific psychology; he also received the first American Psychological Association award for his contributions to professional psychology. His research dating back to the early 1940s, in its simplest form, indicates that when we create psychological climates in which people are free to be what their experience has taught them they are, their behavior is positive and constructive; it is satisfying both to the person and to other people.

Philosophical Assumptions —

What is at question in evaluating the two positions are not matters of fact but assumptions. The facts are that Skinner and Rogers can produce the effects they claim. Which we choose to believe is best for us depends on what we think is the basic nature of man and what we want mankind to become. These are important considerations. We know that to a surprising degree people become what we make them become. The strongest single determiner of how we treat people is our belief about their nature.

If we give people freedom to be responsible and then make it possible for them to respond in responsible ways, their behavior is essentially positive and constructive. If, though, we limit their freedom, believe they are irresponsible, and restrict their behavior, aberrations appear and their behavior becomes negative and destructive.

We know that children reared in homes in which they are not loved and in which their freedom is arbitrarily restricted develop more negative behaviors than children who are reared in loving homes in which their parents help them accept responsibility for their behavior. What sometimes confuses us is the mistaken belief that parents who give their children everything the children desire are loving parents. Loving parents do not deny their children what they need but they do not seek to satisfy every whim. They leave some pleasures for the future. Loving parents help their children learn how to obtain satisfactions for themselves.

Evaluating Skinner's and Rogers' Positions

Rogers' and Skinner's positions lead to predictions which have been tested in numerous studies. When the results are examined, support is found for both of the systems. Thus either system works and can be used as a basis for human relationships. The important question becomes, therefore, "Which system would we want to live under?"

Consistency With Our Basic Tenets —

The two positions can be evaluated through their consequences. One way to do this is by comparing them with our form of government and its purposes. Skinner would object. His position is that we have been conditioned to believe that freedom exists and that it is a worthwhile objective. To him, freedom is a restricting concept which keeps us from achieving more important and worthwhile objectives. His arguments are not convincing to some people. Furthermore, it is our present form of government for which students are being prepared, not some other form. What is done in schools should better prepare students to live in our nation as it is organized. So we ask, "What are the principal bases of our form of government?"

We hold these truths to be self-evident, that all men are created equal; that they are endowed by their Creator with certain unalienable rights; that among these, are life, liberty, and the pursuit of happiness. That, to secure these rights, governments are instituted among men, deriving their just powers from the consent of the governed . . . .

With these thoughts as assumptions, a system of government was established which sought to provide a broadened basis of sovereignty, to the end that each person could have maximum opportunity for self rule; that is, each person would become a sovereign. Because of practical necessity, the form of government was made representative rather than direct; too many people were involved. In addition, some of the founding fathers could not accept the belief that each person could or should be sovereign. As a consequence, many compromises were effected which to some degree limited the basic concept.

To assure that people could make good decisions, a system of compulsory and publicly supported education was established. Low postal rates were encouraged to make dissemination of newspapers and other periodicals possible. Freedom of the press was established so that people could be informed. It was believed that people could exercise their sovereignty intelligently only if they could read and write and were well informed. Public tax-supported education was created to enable people to make intelligent decisions. The first federal effort to support education was through the Northwest Ordinance which became law on July 13, 1787. It stated, "Religion, morality, and knowledge, being necessary to good government and the happiness of mankind, schools and the means of education shall forever be encouraged."

Many people believe that democracy and majority rule are identical and that to vote is to be democratic. We sometimes find even small groups of people deciding issues by voting when there are more appropriate methods available for reaching decisions such as consensus opinion. We vote in our democracy and have majority rule because these are methods by which we can insure the greatest number of people the opportunity to exercise their sovereignty. Democracy is not a form of governmental organization; it is a set of beliefs about the worth and dignity of individual people and their right to govern themselves. We have organized our government so that these beliefs can be implemented and people can be sovereign.

Without doubt, there are flaws in the way we have organized to implement our basic belief about the sovereign rights of people, and we must continue serious effort to improve the organization. But until such time as we believe that there are more important things than the welfare of individual people and their right to govern themselves, we should not change to a form of government consistent with another set of beliefs. While we hold such truths to be self-evident, the job of the schools must be to help people become as effective as possible in exercising their sovereignty.

The role of the schools must be consistent with the role of the government. We cannot teach people how to be free and accept responsibility for their own destinies with an educational system which would limit choice, deprive students of opportunities to practice responsibility for themselves and their education, fail to help them learn how to evaluate their own behavior, and not provide them with opportunities to make wise choices. Learning to be sovereign requires an apprenticeship in the exercise of responsibility. At one time the home took care of this. Since many homes no longer do this, schools have had to fulfill the role. A major purpose of the schools is to help people learn how to accept and exercise responsibility for themselves, and to help them gain the experience needed for making intelligent choices.

It is evident that one of the two teaching roles described earlier is more desirable than the other for achieving the purposes of schools in our democracy. A teacher who seeks to open children to experience, plans with them, helps them monitor their own work, helps them accept responsibility for themselves, and is sensitive to their suggestions and guidance — that is, a teacher who practices a facilitating role — is attempting to teach in a manner consistent with the basic tenets of our country.

The Objective Evidence —

There is another means of evaluating Rogers' and Skinner's positions and the facilitating and controlling teaching role concepts. That is through research evidence such as presented earlier. The conclusions from that evidence are clear; teachers who seek facilitating roles are more successful and have more helpful relationships with their students than those who seek controlling roles.

The evidence supports the assertion that schools are more effective when they attempt to open children to past and new experience and its personal meanings; help them plan their work and studies; assist them in monitoring their own goals and progress; aid them in accepting responsibility for themselves; and remain sensitive to their suggestions and guidance than when they attempt to mold children in the school's image of what is desirable.

The Person We Desire —

The best way to evaluate the opposed philosophies of Rogers and Skinner and the contrasting teaching-role concepts is in terms of what we want schools to do for young people. The first means of evaluation suggested was a comparison of each ideology with the tenets of our government. The second was in terms of how children feel about themselves and other people, about their schools, and other allied concepts.

But the form of our government and the beliefs which led to its establishment might not be that which is best for young people. Even though students have good relationships with their teachers, find their schools and schoolwork meaningful, like their schools, and have parents who like the schools, we cannot be certain that we are doing what is best for them. We cannot be sure what we are doing is consistent with what schools were developed for or what they should do. We need to look at what we want schools to do for youngsters and use this as a criterion for evaluating the two positions. Central to this consideration is the nature of intelligence.

Education and Intelligence

Early in this century we accepted as factual a number of assumptions about the nature of intelligence. The validity of many of these assumptions has now been questioned. Quite possibly some are misleading, and some may actually be harming students by limiting their potential growth.

According to traditional beliefs, intelligence is innate and inherited. It is something young people take to school with them. The amount they have determines how much they will learn. Thus intelligence is assumed to be a "given" in the educational equation. When intelligence is thus construed, attempts to help children are limited. Why spend effort trying to help those who cannot learn very well when an equal amount of time spent with more intelligent children will yield more positive results?

Intelligence need not be thought of as something people take to school with them. It is probably more valid to think of it as something they take home with them. Intelligence can and should be developed in schools. *The principal reason for the existence of schools is the creation of intelligence.*

Intelligence and Behavior —

Parents send their children to school because they believe they will behave more intelligently as a result. Parents often say, "We want our children to be more successful than we were." What they are saying, in a way, is that they want their children to be able to behave more intelligently than they would without an education.

Parents in this country have always supported schools for this purpose. The first tax-supported schools were established so that boys and girls could learn to read. If they could read the

Bible, they could escape sin and damnation. In this way the children would be acting intelligently. The Northwest Ordinance set aside public land to support education so that people could learn the skills necessary for being informed. If they were informed, they could make intelligent decisions in politics and other activities.

The word "intelligence" is being used here to describe the quality of people's behavior. In this sense it is used as an adjective, not a noun. Many people object to such a use. They assume that intelligence is an internal characteristic, presumedly of genetic origin, which people either have or do not have, or have in various degrees. For 70 years they have been taught that this is what intelligence is. It is central to the assumptions they make about people and their nature.

Intelligence can be assumed, though, to be the ability to identify problems and to formulate workable solutions for them. Intelligence includes the ability to suggest solutions to problems and evaluate the effectiveness of the solutions. It involves knowing when a problem has not been solved, and where to go for additional help or information which might solve it.

This way of viewing intelligence is closer to reality than the more commonly accepted belief. When people's intelligence is measured by a test, all that is measured is the quality of their solutions to problems. If their solutions are judged adequate because they are commonly accepted, people are judged intelligent. The supposedly internal quality called intelligence can never be measured directly. What is measured is the quality of people's behavior, and these measurements are used to infer the amount of their "intelligence." All we *ever* have are estimates of the quality of behavior.

Where we go wrong in measuring intelligence is to assume that the quality of a person's behavior tells us something about an internal characteristic called intelligence. To make this inference, it is necessary to make numerous other assumptions such as those described below. Many of these are untenable.

Intelligence and Test Scores —

When intelligence is measured, a test is given. This test has also been given to a large number of people of the same age as the person who is being tested. The person's performance is then compared to others' of the same age to determine if it is superior, similar, or inferior to the performance of this normative group, and the degree to which it differs from the average of the normative group. If the person scores higher than the average person of the same age, he is judged to have above-average intelligence.

Intelligence is usually reported as an IQ, a term which has become something "real" to teachers and parents. There is actually nothing real about it. Intelligence tests are scaled so that a person's score can be compared with the scores of other people who have taken the test. In this way it can be determined how old the average person is who makes a similar score. This age, called mental age is expressed in months and converted into IQ by dividing it by the person's chronological (calendar) age, also expressed in months. The result is multiplied by 100 to rid it of the decimal point. This is called an intelligence quotient or IQ [3].

The process of measuring intelligence assumes that intelligence can be measured by seeing how much a person has learned. If the person has learned more than the average person of the same age, he is said to be more intelligent than the average person and his IQ is greater than 100. Most psychologists agree that intelligence tests are only very general measures of achievement.

An understanding of intelligence seems simple until we begin to ask certain questions and examine the many assumptions involved in its measurement. In the first place, how can we link a child's performance on an "intelligence" test to a supposedly innate characteristic? To do so requires that we assume a characteristic called intelligence. We have then to further assume that it is inherited. This is easy to do since ability to learn in school seems to "run" in families; some families enjoy more success, fortune, and fame. So we conclude that some families have superior genes for intelligence. An "intelligence" test may ask a question such as "How many people are there at a birthday party which includes a man, his wife, their two sons, and each of the sons' three children?" What is there about the answers to such questions that leads us to believe that we are testing a genetic characteristic? All we have is an estimate of the person's ability to solve the problem which is then assumed to reflect the amount of his intelligence.

Most people believe that intelligence tests have been proved to measure intelligence. This is a reasonable but invalid belief. No standard exists against which the results of intelligence tests can be compared. Such comparisons can be made with weights and measures, for example, by comparing them with standard sets of weights and measures kept at the National Bureau of Standards. But no standard measure of intelligence exists, so the results of intelligence tests cannot be compared with it.

Two methods have been used to "validate" tests of intelligence. In the first, people are measured with the test and the results compared with their scores on a previously accepted test of intelligence. This validates the new test only if the older test has been validated, which has not been done with any test. If there was an effort to validate the older test, it was by comparing it with a previous test and that in turn had never been validated.

The second means of "validating" intelligence tests, the one which has been used most often, employs what is called a developmental criterion. To validate a test by this means, it is first given to a large number of children. If scores show progressive increases with increases in the ages of the children, the test is said to be developmentally valid. Such a conclusion rests on a number of hidden assumptions. For example, how do we know that what is being tested is not school achievement?

Validation Against a Prior Test —

The first of the two methods used to "validate" intelligence tests grew from the work of the Frenchman Alfred Binet. Binet was commissioned to develop a means of identifying children who would have difficulty learning in the schools of Paris, France. He developed a series of scales which proved to be somewhat effective for this purpose. Binet, however, never claimed that he was measuring intelligence. To the contrary, he prescribed courses in "mental orthopedics" for those who scored low on his scales so that their scores could be raised and their chances for success in school bettered. In his report, Binet included a chapter on "The Training of Intelligence" which began with a rejection of the notion proposed by "some recent philosophers" that "the intelligence of an individual is a fixed quantity, a quantity which one cannot augment" by saying, "We must protest and react against this brutal pessimism."

In spite of his disclaimer, translators and importers of Binet's work such as Lewis Terman at Leland Stanford University, Henry Goddard at the Vineland, New Jersey, Training School, and Robert Yerkes at Harvard proclaimed that the Binet test provided a measure of "innate intelligence" although there were no data to support the assertion.

At a later date the concept of IQ was invented and applied to the scores of Binet-like tests. It was opinion and assumption which led to the conclusions that Binet had measured intelligence and that intelligence was innate and heritable. Leon J. Kamin of Princeton University [4] rejects such reasoning since it places those who question the validity of IQ tests as measures of innate intelligence on the defensive; that is, it forces those who disagree to prove that intelligence is *not* innate and heritable. He points out that it is incumbent on people who make an assertion to present evidence to support it, not for the questioners to present evidence to refute it. In fact, the nature of science makes it impossible to prove that something does not exist. Science is a system of thinking which seeks evidence for the support of ideas or hypotheses; and unless it can demonstrate support for a hypothesis, it must reject it. In assertions about the nature of intelligence, the logic of science has been bypassed.

Binet's scale was never validated as a measure of intelligence. Neither were its English translations or modifications of these. How can these, then, serve as standards against which to compare other tests which purport to measure intelligence?

The Developmental Criterion —

The second method for "validating" an intelligence test uses a developmental criterion. This criterion assumes that if children make progressively higher scores on a test as they increase in age, the test is a valid measure of intelligence. To accept this, a number of additional assumptions must be made. For example, it is necessary to assume that all of the children who are being measured by the test have had equal opportunity to be familiar with the test materials. If they have not, differences in scores may be due only to differences in opportunity.

The assumption of equality of opportunity is a condition which can *never* be met. It helps explain why numerous studies in the 1920s and 1930s showed ridiculous results such as, for example, city children have higher IQs than country children, northerners have higher IQs than southerners, white children have higher average IQs than black children, and children of college professors are above average in IQ. It is true that white, northern, city children did have higher average "intelligence" test scores, but they also had better opportunity to be familiar with the test materials. Suffice to say, all children taking an IQ test have not had equal opportunity to be familiar with the test materials. These differences in opportunity are reflected in differences in test scores.

To try to satisfy the requirement that all children have equal opportunity to be acquainted with the test materials, materials have been selected which, it is hoped, are either within the range of experience of all of the children or out of the range of experience of any of the children. This is probably impossible. Many materials favor children from more affluent homes. None of the materials favor poor children because they are out of the range of their experience. In recent years, many of the materials on intelligence tests have been included in children's games, and the children of more affluent families have had greater access to them. It is doubtful that the familiarity requirement can be fulfilled.

Another assumption in establishing developmental validity is that all people who are being measured by the test have been equally challenged to learn what is on the test. This is particularly important on paper-and-pencil tests of "intelligence" where the questions often deal with things like those taught in school. The assumption holds that if the children have all been exposed to the same materials, those who have learned the most are the most intelligent. But we know, for example, that girls are often challenged to do better in school than are boys, and that because of their greater verbal maturity when they enter school, girls learn more rapidly than boys. The measured IQs of girls are higher on the average than boys, probably because of this difference.

People who live in a world like that of many black children and poor children may not try very hard to succeed in school because "what difference will it make?" Without doubt the children of educated parents are more highly motivated to learn in school than the children of poorly educated parents. Educated parents read more and have more reading materials around their homes. When their relationships with their children are good, their children want to be like them. It is not surprising that children who do well on paper-and-pencil tests of intelligence also do well in school. It is doubtful that the assumption of equal motivation to learn can ever be satisfied.

Another assumption in developmental validity is equality of reading ability. When we use paper-and-pencil tests of intelligence, we assume that all of the children are able to read the test with equal capability. Otherwise the test becomes one of reading, not of intelligence. But many children are unable to read the tests so they score poorly on them. Such children are labeled "retarded," which is then given as a reason for their not being able to learn very well! A few years ago I subjected some junior high school children's "mental maturity" scores and their scores from an allied achievement test to a factor analysis. The most significant factor which emerged was reading. If the children could read, they could score higher on both the test of mental maturity *and* on the achievement tests.

Another assumption basic to developmental validity is that all people taking an "intelligence" test are equally motivated to do well on it. That is expecting a lot. How many people have had an experience such as I had in high school? My classmates and I were lined up for something which obviously was special. Then a rumor started which said that "they" were going to find out how smart we were. If we scored high on the test, "they" would expect more out of us in school. Although I was a good student, I did not want "them" to expect any more from me and I took the test with this in mind.

When I entered the army in World War II, I was given the Army General Classification Test (AGCT) which supposedly measures intelligence. Duty assignments are based, in part, on the scores soldiers make on the test. I was much more highly motivated to score high on this test than on the one I took in high school.

How many children are not motivated to do their best on intelligence tests simply because they do not care? Our schools contain many who do not enjoy the kind of learning they encounter in school, and who believe that achieving well in school is not worth the effort or that it will not get them where they want to go.

The Innateness of Intelligence —

If intelligence is innate, it should remain constant throughout life. Much data exist to show that this is just not so.

In the 1920s and 1930s, many studies questioned the constancy of intelligence or of IQ. For example, it was reported that the longer children remain in orphanages, the lower their IQs become. Too, it was discovered that if children from orphanages are placed in good foster homes, their IQs increase; and if they are later returned to the orphanages, their IQs again decrease. The English psychologist, Hugh Gordon, studied canal-boat and gypsy children. He found that the longer children remain in such poorly stimulating environments, the lower are their IQs. When Professor E. J. Asher was at the University of Kentucky in the 1930s, he measured the IQs of mountain children and found the same thing.

The Veracity of Some Key Studies —

Questions about the validity of intelligence tests and their assumptions have been raised by several workers in the field.

One of these is Leon J. Kamin, who shared the findings of his investigations in *The Science and Politics of IQ* [4]. Kamin is chairman of the Department of Psychology at Princeton University. His book raised serious questions about the methods used by early investigators in the field of intelligence, especially casting serious doubt on the integrity of the noted English psychologist Sir Cyril Burt. Burt was knighted for his work with twins which led to the commonly held belief that intelligence is heritable. Kamin's questions led London's *Sunday Times'* medical correspondent, Oliver Gillie, to investigate their plausibility. What he found is reported in the *APA Monitor* for December, 1976 [5].

Gillie's discoveries raised further questions. He concluded that Burt probably presented faked data, or at least "slotted in" data to already published work, to substantiate his claims about the heritability of intelligence. Burt may even have invented fictitious collaborators to further his notions. His conclusion that 85 per cent of an individual's performance on IQ tests is attributable to inherited characteristics cannot be accepted because of his questionable data and methods of collecting them. Neither can the conclusions of Arthur Jensen be accepted without question. Jensen has been responsible for the recent resurgence of the notion of the heritability of IQ and the inferiority of black intelligence. Some of his major conclusions rest on data and conclusions which are Burt's.

Nevertheless, little attention has been paid to Burt's exposure and to its implications for recently published work in this country. Nor has much attention been paid to newer studies of intelligence which do not bear out the concept of heritability such as those of R. B. Zajonc, a professor of psychology at the University of Michigan. Zajonc's work [6] was originally published in *Science*, the official publication of the American Association for the Advancement of Science. AAAS gave Zajonc and his co-worker Gregory B. Markus their Socio-Psychological Prize for 1975 for their work.

American psychology and American education seem to have a need to believe that intelligence is heritable and that the amount of intelligence people inherit determines how much they can learn. What is being questioned here are concepts such as the heritability of IQ, the constancy of IQ, and the measurement of an innate something called intelligence by means of intelligence tests. These have been asserted to be truths but there is no evidence to support them. Until such evidence is presented, we should stick closer to the facts.

And what are these facts? What we measure when we use intelligence tests is the quality of people's problem-solving behavior as judged by commonly accepted solutions to the problems posed by the tests. To go beyond this without supporting data is to lose scientific objectivity and probably to harm children.

Intelligence and Schooling —

The implication of the belief that intelligence tests measure the quality of people's behavior is important. If I ask a teacher, "Do you think you can change a person's intelligence?" the teacher probably will reply "No." If, though, I ask the teacher, "Do you think you can change the quality of a child's behavior? the teacher will respond with an emphatic "Yes!" Teachers will say, "We can take children who cannot respond intelligently to a book and we can help them learn to read the book." Or they will say, "We can take children who don't know how to do math or a lot of other things and we can teach them how to do these things, or at least we can help them learn how to do these things." People who have learned how to read or how to work mathematics problems behave more intelligently than people who have not learned these things, especially in situations which require these understandings. A person who can read can respond more intelligently to an application form than one who cannot read it. Children who know algebra are able to solve problems which mathematical geniuses could not solve before its formulation. *Schools exist to create intelligence.*

This changes the focus. If schools exist to create intelligence, we must ask, "What influences the intellectual quality of behavior?" There are a lot of answers to this question. Poorly informed people cannot respond as intelligently as well-informed people in many situations, so information and cognitive skills are important determiners of intelligence. It is often assumed, therefore, that knowledge is the *only* factor with which the schools should be concerned. However, attitudes, values, self-concepts, study skills, skill in human relationships, experience, and openness to experience and its meanings are also important determiners of the quality of people's behavior and their intelligence.

If intelligence is a quality of behavior and if schools exist to change behavior, then what roles should teachers assume? If schools wish to change the content of what children know, they can practice controlling teaching role concepts. There is no doubt but that good teachers working in this framework can help children learn school subjects. But if schools wish to change what children know *and* how they behave, they must encourage facilitating roles.

References

1. APA 84th Annual Convention Program — September 3-September 7, 1976. p xix-xx.

2. Rogers, C. R. & Skinner, B. F. Some issues concerning the control of human behavior. Unpublished debate, Chicago, 64th Annual Convention of the American Psychological Association, September 1956.

3. In recent years, some test constructors have recognized the problems involved in defining intelligence and the lack of validation of intelligence tests. Because of this, they have tended to say that "intelligence is what this test measures," and to speak in terms of academic aptitude rather than intelligence. There has also been a trend away from computing IQs by comparing a child's age with the age of children who make similar scores. In such cases, a deviation IQ is computed in which a child's score is compared with the average score of children of the same age. This, however, does not entirely resolve the problem of developmental validity. Furthermore, even though deviation scores are reported (as in the SAT) by test constructors, many of these same constructors continue to use the term IQ.

4. Kamin, L. J. *The Science and Politics of IQ.* New York: John Wiley and Sons, 1974.

5. The Burt affair...Sleuthing in science. Washington: *APA Monitor.* 7:12, December, 1976, p 1, 4.

6. Zajonc, R. B. Family configuration and intelligence. *Science,* 192: 4236, April 16, 1976, 227-236.

Chapter Eleven

Beliefs:
The Roots of Behavior

If the goal of the schools is to help people behave intelligently, schools must become more concerned with influencing students' behavior. This introduces important philosophical problems.

Schools have always been interested in changing students' behavior but their attempts to help children behave intelligently have centered mostly around helping them become well informed. The traditional concern of schools with the behavior of children has been with controlling the behavior of *problem* children.

There are good philosophical reasons why schools have sought to avoid behavioral control. School personnel do not believe, for example, they have a right to control students' lives even if the control supposedly is for the students' own good. Schools in our country believe that they exist to free people, not to control their lives. In addition, teachers believe that they can change students' behavior only by negative means such as coercion, indoctrination, bribery, shame, and other similar practices. They are reluctant to use such methods and when they do, they try to call them by different names.

In spite of teachers' protests that they do not use such procedures, many students report, for example, that their teachers try to shame them into changing their behavior. Although teachers do not approve of bribing students, they sometimes use grades for this purpose. They, however, more often use grades to punish children for wrongdoings, usually with the hope that students will change as a consequence.

Although its practitioners reject the term "bribe," behavior modification uses a system of rewards which more properly should be called bribes. Behavior modification is currently used to train children in schools for the mentally retarded, to elicit desired behavior from patients in state mental hospitals, and to teach slow-learning children. It is a direct outgrowth of B. F. Skinner's theory of operant conditioning. As practiced in schools, behavior modification rewards students whenever they behave or attempt to behave as their teachers desire with things much as M&M candies or with tokens that can be exchanged for prizes or other rewards. Supposedly, through the application of behavior modification, the behavior of students is conditioned much like the bar-pressing behavior of rats. The use of behavior modification with retarded people who cannot control their behavior is more easily justified than is its use with more normal people. Many teachers reject its use with students who are capable of exercising self-control.

A recent attempt to improve students' learning used systematic extrinsic rewards throughout an entire school. If the children learned what they were supposed to learn, they were given tokens which could be traded for prizes. The prizes ranged in value from candy bars to items such as color television sets. An evaluation of the project showed that there was no reason to believe that children had learned more under this method of instruction than they would have been expected to learn under more traditional procedures.

Indoctrination is another way of altering students' behavior. However, indoctrination in schools is viewed as unacceptable by many people in our society — although the one-sided points of view which students are sometimes given in their classrooms can be classed only as indoctrination. Few teachers believe that schools should indoctrinate; they are not aware that they do it at times.

If teachers cannot coerce or shame or bribe students into changing their behavior, and if the goals of schools must be behavioral change, then how can schools get children to change? Fortunately, an alternative way of helping students change is available. To understand it, we must first look at why people behave as they do. From this we can get clues about how we can help them behave more intelligently.

What Determines Our Behavior?

What each of us does is consistent with our beliefs about the world in which we live; believing is behaving. Although our behavior may be difficult to understand by another person who has different beliefs about the world, it seems intelligible to us. Other people may believe that we are peculiar for doing many of the things we do, but they make sense to us. If others could see the world as we do, our behavior would make sense to them, too.

Suppose we watch people walk down the street. We might wonder why they walk around ladders. We could conclude that players on a winning high school basketball team have poor habits of hygiene because they wear dirty shirts. We might even wonder if "Bear" Bryant is too poor to buy more than one hat since that is all we may have seen him wear during a particular football season. We would more likely reach such conclusions if we do not know that such practices are believed by many people to ward off bad luck. Members of a winning ball club sometimes believe that it will break their winning "streak" if they wash their suits, and many people believe that walking under a ladder brings bad luck. Professional baseball players are a super-stitious group. Observe the way they behave as they go out onto the field or when they return to the dugout.

When we see the world through the eyes of other people, their behavior is understandable. If you observe me, you may believe that I am behaving peculiarly. If you could see the world from my point of view, however, you would be surprised if I acted differently. Suppose we watch someone behave in a certain way and then we ask, "Why did you do that?" The response probably will be a surprised look and a reply, "Why, what would you have done?" *All behavior is determined by and strictly pertinent to the world as the behaver sees it at the instant of action* [1].

Belief and Behavior —

If I believe that demons or devils cause disease, I will cover my mouth when I yawn to keep them from jumping in. If I become ill, I will believe that I am inhabited by demons; and I will understand when people around me begin making loud noises, wearing frightening masks, and creating bad odors that they are trying to drive out the demons and devils which are causing me to be sick. It will not occur to me that disease may not be caused by demons and devils, and my behavior will be consistent with my beliefs.

When people believed that the earth was flat, they avoided the edges. When they believed that phrenology could help them, they had their heads examined. Many of the most cherished beliefs people hold today are similar in nature. Sometime in the future, people will look back at us today and laugh. But even if a belief is invalid, it still affects us. For example, a friend of mine relates that when he assumed that the commonly held belief that wet feet causes colds was true, he found many examples to prove it to himself. But when research gave him evidence to question the assumption, he began to find as many examples in the opposite direction.

In the nineteenth century, there was a commonly held belief that a fetus or a child was a homunculus or miniature adult. You may have observed the effect of this belief in operation. For example, the illustrations for Lewis Carroll's *Alice in Wonderland and Through the Looking Glass* show Alice with a child's body and an adult head. You can find this phenomenon in portraits of children and dolls of the same period. Our beliefs influence our perceptions. We see things as we believe they are. Our behavior is consistent with our perceptions; as we see, so do we behave.

A study which a former student, Bob McGee, and I did gives a good example of the effect of belief on behavior [2]. That study shows that students who have positive attitudes toward psychology perform more effectively in a learning experiment than those who have negative attitudes. Bob and I asked students to learn pairs of Finnish words and their English equivalents. We also measured their attitudes toward psychology. There is no relationship between their attitudes and their original learning of the pairs of words, but their retention of the word pairs is significantly influenced. What students learn in the experiment is retained more fully if they believe things such as, "Psychological experiments are useful and will eventually help us to completely understand people." and "Psychology, in general, is a valuable, quantitative science with many practical applications." On the other hand, they forget rapidly if they hold beliefs such as, "Psychological experiments are a total waste of time," and "Psychology, in general, is nothing but a witch hunt."

A second characteristic of people is that they change their beliefs slowly. This is the principle of perceptual constancy. The church of their youth and the first political party to which they gave allegience tend to continue to be their choices. The methods used in rearing us continue to be seen by us as the best. We believe our children will be helped most by the same content and methods of education that we thought were helpful to us.

Perceptual constancy is a basic psychological principle. People ascribe constancy to their environments so they can exist. We learn the color of an object in shadow, and it appears the same to us in sunlight or on various backgrounds even though its stimulus effect on the retinas of our eyes is different. As an object approaches us or as we approach it, we see it as constant in size although the size of its retinal image changes. Even though railroad tracks appear to converge in the distance, we see them as parallel. The survival value of such a characteristic cannot be overemphasized. We recognize water regardless of its context, the time of day, or the shape of its container. We can judge the size of an animal in spite of its distance from us, or other factors.

We also maintain consistency in our perceptions of ourselves. We see ourselves in similar ways regardless of the context of our actions. If as children we steal from a candy shelf, it is only to be "like the other kids," not because we are dishonest. Love and charity are good ideals and we can believe that we still have them even when we are being "shrewd business people." When children are caught cheating on tests, many of them say, "I didn't want to fail." To fail would require a new concept or definition of self.

If we think of the Dutch as quaint people with wooden shoes, windmills, and dikes, our ideas may change significantly when we are given new information, although we may revert gradually to our original ideas when the pressures to change have been removed. Our attitudes toward Eskimos and Indians probably have changed little from those we formed in elementary school, despite our more mature knowledge. The images we hold of God usually are not different from those we held when we were children.

Thus behavior is influenced by our personal beliefs, and these change slowly. Factors other than beliefs also affect our perceptions and through them our behavior. These factors include things such as needs, values, physiological conditions, threat, opportunity, and concepts of self and other people. Each of these causes perceptions to be personal in nature.

Need and Perception —

When hungry people are shown a dimly lit out-of-focus picture, they usually see food in it. Thirsty people are more apt to see beverages. And when frustrated people are shown words at a rate so rapid that they cannot read them, their guesses are more often aggressive words than would be expected if they were not frustrated.

Professor Charles E. Osgood recounts, "An office that I pass each day is numbered 400D; inevitably, when the hour is near mealtime, I perceive this as FOOD. The car I used to drive had the euphemistic label SILVER STREAK on its dashboard; inevitably, when the hour was near mealtime, I would read this as SILVER STEAK [3]."

When my parents and I were on trips, around noontime my father would become interested in signs advertising foods and restaurants. He usually denied that hunger prompted his response, contending that it was the quality of the sign or of the restaurant. Needless to say, we did not believe him.

Values and Perceptions —

Similarly, values are determinants of our perceptions and behavior. In a study, I discovered that students who value people in ways similar to those of their instructors make higher marks in their classes than students with different values, even though their marks are based on objective tests derived solely from textbooks [4].

Value causes children to overestimate the size of coins. The amount of overestimation is directly related to the value of the coin. Poor children make larger overestimations than rich children. Likewise, children from lower socio-economic groups have greater discrepancies between their performance on tasks and their estimates of their future performances than children from higher socio-economic groups. They also are less realistic in recalling their performances.

When people are asked to guess at words flashed rapidly on a screen, their guesses are in the direction of words which have high value for them. The first words they can distinguish when the projection times are increased are those which have high value for them. The last words they recognize are those with low value.

Physiology and Perception —

Another factor of importance in our perceptions is our physiological condition. A person with a malfunctioning central nervous system cannot form or change perceptions as readily as one whose system is functioning properly. Similarly, a sleepy child will not perceive the same way as a wide-awake child. Metabolic factors, endocrine disturbances, and narcotic chemicals affect perceptions. Our spouses and children know that we will hold different perceptions when sitting relaxed after dinner than immediately upon arriving home after a hard day's work.

Regretfully, many children are being given reduced opportunities for success in school because of physiological factors which their parents could control if they would. Children are often kept up after they should be in bed. They are allowed to stay up longer than advisable to watch television programs. In small homes, parents keep children awake by viewing television after the children are in bed. These children (often the majority in a classroom) are unable to profit from their school experience the next day to the degree they should be able to. And who gets the blame? The teachers and the schools. Children in the lower elementary grades need as much as 11 or 12 hours sleep each night to be able to function optimally.

Similar things can be said about the diets of children. The average child today is overweight, which is not only harmful but a cause of poor school learning. Such children are sluggish physically and mentally. They cannot do their best work in school. The blame for children's weight problems must be placed on their parents. The diet of the average child contains far more fat and refined carbohydrates (especially sugar) than it should. Parents find it more convenient, though, to have dinner at a fast-food restaurant than to prepare adequate, well-balanced meals at home, especially if they have been working all day and are exhausted.

If parents cannot control their children's bedtime or diets, they can at least stop blaming the schools for students' poor learning. The decline in SAT scores which has been so widely decried is small. So small, in fact, that we need look no further than the poor physiological condition of school age children to explain it [5].

Intelligence is directly affected by the physical state of a person. This is so because the ability to form adequate perceptions is affected by the physical state. If people do not form adequate perceptions, their behavior will be inadequate and thus unintelligent. Many factors affect physiological functioning, and others can produce anatomical changes in neural structure. For example, the ability to behave intelligently can be reduced by damage to the physical self, by toxic or chemical poisons, and by physiological malfunctions such as endocrine disturbances. The potential for intelligent behavior is greater at birth than at any later point in life for most people.

Experience and Perception —

The perceptual field is constructed from experience and its personal meanings. Children are born with little experience.

Such experience as they have at birth consists of tactile and auditory sensations to which they have been exposed and kinesthetic experience from their own movements and those of their mothers. Children are born into a confusion of stimuli and are unable to differentiate stimuli except those that are compelling or overwhelming.

Infants differentiate stimuli from the contexts in which they occur, but they differentiate only those which have meaning for their organisms. This process of differentiation is called learning. Infants give positive reactions to food and they attempt to incorporate it. They react to other stimuli only when the stimuli are intense. Loud noises and bright lights elicit apprehension. Intense stimuli are probably meaningful because they are painful, and infants are startled by them.

As infants mature they have other experiences. These react on them at an organic or physical level. Some experiences are seen to have personal meaning because they have value for the organism. They are seen as contributing to its survival, growth, or pleasure. Other experiences are used to form attitudes and values.

Without personal meaning, experience has little or no effect on the structure of the perceptual field. This can be illustrated by studies in the area of "latent learning." If a hungry rat is placed in a simple "T" maze which has food in one arm and water in the other, the rat will explore the maze and find the food. In doing so, it may pass the water. Eventually, the rat will learn where the food is and go to it without turning into the wrong arm. If we now feed the rat and withhold water and again place it in the maze, the rat will take as long to learn where the water is as it took it to learn where the food was. The water did not have meaning when it was experienced.

This phenomenon is not limited to rats. Have you ever driven along a stretch of interstate highway and run out of gas? If so, you asked yourself, "How far back was the last filling station?" Could you remember? Probably not unless there was something about the filling station which called it to your attention, for example, the price of its gasoline. If the price of the gasoline was especially high or low, it may have had meaning for you. After you have once run out of gas on an interstate highway, you may be acutely aware of all of the service stations and you may even glance at your gas gauge when you pass them. Service stations on interstate highways now have personal meaning for you.

Here is another example. You are driving on a road which passes through a town you have never seen before. After you leave the town, your companion asks you if you have anything for a headache. You do not have anything so you ask yourself, "Was there a drugstore in the town we just passed?" You probably cannot remember even if you looked directly at one. It would have no personal meaning for you at the time unless you are a pharmacist or for some other personal reason.

Schools seek to give people experience in things they will "need" to know to function adequately. Without these experiences, people cannot behave intelligently in situations which require the experience. Unfortunately, much of the experience students get in school has little personal meaning for them. Thus it is either forgotten or they are unable to use it when they need it. Schools believe that latent learning occurs even if what is learned is not meaningful. So they seek to give students information *now* so that when it is needed in the future they will have it. Significant learning (that which changes behavior) does not occur in this way. Let me illustrate.

After I received my bachelor's degree in chemistry, I applied for a job in analysis with a chemical manufacturing company. In the job interview I was asked many things. One of these was, "If you were given a compound that would not dissolve in any of the usual reagents, what would you do?" The question stumped me. When we had analyzed such substances in class, it had been a meaningless laboratory exercise. I needed to know the answer only to pass the course. After I finished the course, it lost its meaning. When the interviewer told me the answer to his question and asked me if I had ever heard of such a process, I recalled it and at that moment it had meaning for me. I still remember the question and its answer.

It is relatively easy to get children to discover personal meanings in much of what they are learning in elementary schools. This can be done readily in such subjects as reading or elementary school mathematics. To help a child find meaning in reading, first find something the child wants or needs to read. One way of doing this is by having the child dictate a story to the teacher. The teacher then writes it down and helps the child learn how to read it. This is a frequent approach to reading used in the schools.

If a child has to discover the personal meaning of reading from most elementary reading books, such meaning may never be discovered. Many reading books have meaningless content for the children who will read them. This is true for both boys and girls and the children of poor parents. Girls have often been depicted as standing around applauding as boys have adventures. This has been true to such a degree that neither girls nor boys wanted to read stories about girls. On the other hand, the boys who are depicted in reading books are not the masculine type with which boys want to identify.

Arithmetic can be given meaning through experience. If children have to make purchases in a store or they have to make change, they rapidly learn the arithmetic involved. My elder daughter could not work simple arithmetic problems with abstract numbers which were meaningless to her. When I prefaced the numbers with $ signs, her difficulty disappeared. Four-year-old street children in Latin America who beg for money or sell Chiclets have no problem in making change; it has personal meaning.

In our schools, teachers fail to teach children what they need to know if they fail to help children find personal meaning in what they are being asked to learn. It is difficult for teachers to see this since many children discover personal meanings for themselves in what is being taught. The fact that they have discovered personal meanings is not easy for teachers to see. The teachers find what is being taught meaningful to them, and they believe it is meaningful to all of the children.

In our high schools, students who decide to become science or mathematics majors in college find personal meaning in these subjects. They find them easier to learn than students who are in the courses only because they are required. Chemistry is relatively easy for prospective pharmacists to learn; or at least it is easier for them to learn than for people who do not intend to become pharmacists. In colleges which require that all students study chemistry, those who find meaning in the subject such as prospective chemists, pharmacists, and physicians find it easier to learn it than those who do not intend to use it later. Experienced teachers who return to college for graduate study often find meaning in their studies which was absent when they were undergraduate students. Consequently their graduate grade point averages far exceed their undergraduate standings.

Experience is one of the most important determiners of perception. From experience we gain our beliefs about the nature of reality. And it is in terms of these beliefs that we behave. Whether these beliefs are "factual," mythical, or superstitious has little if anything to do with our willingness to act on them. What is superstition to one person may be a strongly held tenet of another person's religion. What is fact to one person may be superstition to another. Combs, Richards, and Richards say, "To each of us the perceptual field of another person contains much error and illusion; it seems an interpretation of reality rather than reality itself. But to each individual his phenomenal field *is* reality; it is the only reality he can know [6]."

Self-Concept and Perception —

The most important of the factors which determine perceptions is the self-concept — the beliefs each of us has about what we are like. All experience is filtered through the self-concept. New experience becomes an integral part of the perceptual field only if it is consistent with the self-concept. If the experience is inconsistent with the self-concept, it may be distorted to help it become consistent and then it can be accepted. Otherwise it is rejected. Have you ever sat in a group discussion where the group was trying to establish new directions? Sometimes a person broaches an idea which threatens to split the group apart. As the discussion continues, though, the idea begins to gain adherents. At this point one of the people who originally rejected the idea may say something like, "Well, what is being suggested is really nothing new," and then go on to explain how the idea is consistent with the group's previous belief. The inconsistent perception has been modified so that it can be accepted. Individuals do the same thing.

Self-concepts are the characteristic ways in which we perceive ourselves. Our behavior is consistent with them. If, for example, I believe I am a poor reader, I will act in a manner consistent with my belief. I will avoid reading and thus I will not get much practice. If I am called on to read in school, the teacher will perceive that I am a poor reader and probably tell me so. This only confirms what I already knew. So, avoiding reading whenever possible, I will never become a good reader. In this way my concept of myself is confirmed.

If I believe that I am likeable, I will be friendly and warm toward people when we meet. But if I believe that people do not like me, I avoid meeting them. Worse still, I may press for people's friendship and to be seen as likeable, doing things which I hope will win their friendship but which may cause me to be rejected. When this happens, my original ideas about myself are reinforced.

If I believe that I am a poor public speaker, I will refuse invitations to speak. On those occasions when I have to talk in front of other people, I will not perform very well and my beliefs about my ability as a public speaker will be confirmed. Sometimes I may be successful but as this is inconsistent with my belief about myself, I will search for reasons to explain my success — reasons which will not cause me to change my perceptions of myself. "The topic was easy." "I did better than usual." "You were really a good audience." "I knew the speech so well it was automatic (not really me)." Such beliefs help me to maintain my perception of myself.

Many surprising relationships have been discovered between self-perceptions and behavior. A study I made [7] shows that people who have low acceptance of themselves report, on the average, twice as many physical complaints as people who are high in acceptance of themselves. For example, low self-accepting people report many more colds than people who have higher self-acceptance. (Perhaps low self-accepting people only believe they have more colds or pay more attention to them.) People with low self-acceptance blame themselves for their unhappiness in life whereas people with higher self-acceptance blame themselves, circumstances, other people, or a combination of these. And if people in a group are permitted to introduce themselves in a "random" order, the last people to do so will be those with low self-acceptance.

Another study confirmed the belief that when given tasks to perform, people with low self-acceptance underestimate their performance more than people with higher self-acceptance [8]. In addition, when people with low self-acceptance are asked to comment on their performance, they feel negatively about it and blame themselves. People with higher acceptance of self feel better about their performance. They blame external circumstances for failure or realistically blame themselves. When people with low self-acceptance are asked to recall their performance at a later date, they underestimate it. People with higher self-acceptance are either correct in their recall or overestimate it.

And in still another study, I found that people who see a sizeable discrepancy between what they are and what they would like to be are less accepting of themselves and show more signs of depression than people who see less discrepancy between what they are and what they would like to be [9].

The things people do are their responses to reality as they perceive it. Our perceptions are influenced by many factors including needs, values, physiological status, experience, and beliefs about what we and other people are like. Perception is to a large measure a private matter influenced by our own beliefs about the nature of the world in which we live.

One implication of this is that if schools want to change students' behavior, they must concentrate on what the students believe is "reality." If schools want to create intelligently behaving people, they cannot afford to concentrate only on students' beliefs about what is real and ignore personal meanings and other factors which control their perceptions.

References

1. Combs, A. W., Richards, A. C. and Richards, F. *Perceptual Psychology*. New York: Harper and Row, 1976, p 18.
2. Bills, R. E. and McGee, C. R. The effect of attitude toward psychology in a learning experiment. *Journal of Personality*. 23: 1955, 499-500.
3. Osgood, C. E. *Method and Theory in Experimental Psychology*. New York: Oxford University Press, 1953.
4. Bills, R. E. The effect of a value on learning. *Journal of Personality*. 21: 1952, 217-222.
5. We have heard much about the decline in achievement of school children as measured by changes in Scholastic Aptitude Test (SAT) scores. When the sizes of these changes are examined, it is seen that the changes are small. There are two types of scores involved, raw scores and percentile scores. By themselves, the raw scores have little meaning. Their meaning emerges when they are converted to percentile scores. The raw scores of the SAT have changed to a noticeable degree during the past several years but their equivalent percentile scores have changed little. The so-called decline is much smaller than the public has been led to believe.
6. Combs, A. W., Richards, A. C. and Richards, F. *Perceptual Psychology*. New York: Harper and Row, 1976, p 24.
7. Bills, R. E. *About People and Teaching*. Lexington: University of Kentucky, Bureau of School Service, 1955.
8. Bills, R. E. A Comparison of scores on the Index of Adjustment and Values with behavior in level of aspiration tasks. *Journal of Consulting Psychology*. 17: 1953, 206-212.
9. Bills, R. E. Rorschach characteristics of persons scoring high and low in acceptance of self. *Journal of Consulting Psychology*. 17: 1953, 36-38.

Chapter Twelve

Perceptual Theory:
Why Students Act
The Way They Do

Behavior is consistent with the world of reality as behavers see it at the instant of action. To understand behavior, we must ask, what do behavers hope to accomplish by their behavior? What determines their choices?

Answers to these questions help us know more about the nature of the school experiences students need. They also explain why the information contained in the data base [1] we are using was collected. There is a rationale called perceptual theory which binds together such things as self-concept, classroom decision-making, the relationship qualities of teachers, parents' and students' feelings about schools, the ideal role concepts of teachers, and the openness of teachers to their experience. This rationale also shows that the major purpose of schooling should be *education for intelligence*.

The First Assumption

Perceptual theory has two basic postulates. The first, already discussed, says that all behavior is determined by and pertinent to the perceptual field of the behaver at the instant of action [2]. This means that people respond to the world as they perceive it at the instant they behave. Seeing is behaving.

This assumption contrasts sharply with the assumption of many psychologists that behavior is a result of stimulation. Stimulus-response psychology, of which Skinner's point of view is one outgrowth, holds that we are stimulated to behave. If our behavior is rewarded or reinforced, the next time we are presented with the same stimulus we will tend to react to it in the same way. Psychologists who accept this point of view see people as passive reactors who react when stimulated. Their position is not debatable since it is an assumption. As already pointed out, if you start with this assumption you can build a logical system of psychology.

Perceptual theorists picture each of us as having a perceptual field which represents the world of reality. The perceptual field is the only reality we can know. It is to this field that we respond rather than to stimuli from outside ourselves. We respond to outside stimuli but only after these become a part of our perceptual fields. In contrast to the behaviorists' position that the human organism is a passive reactor, perceptionists assert that the human organism is capable of self-initiated behavior and of acting upon its environment. This capacity for self-initiated behavior is called self-actualization. People are self-starters.

Because behavior is determined by and pertinent to the structure of the perceptual field at the instant of action, it becomes important to ask, "What determines the structure of the field?" The content of our perceptual fields has been discussed. It consists of experience and its meanings. As we will see, how this content is arranged at any one instant is a function of needs, values, attitudes, physiological status, threat, and other factors. Of these, threat is the most important.

The Second Assumption

The first assumption holds that at the instant of action we are presented with a dynamic field upon which we must act. Thus at the instant of action we are always presented with choices, and we must take action in light of these choices. What determines which action we choose? The second postulate answers this question. All behavior, without exception, is designed to maintain or to enhance our organisms [2]. From the choices which are presented by our perceptual fields at the instant of action, we must choose that which we believe will be most enhancing to our self-organization. If the choice is unimportant to us, we may choose only to maintain self-organization.

The second assumption seems simple enough until we begin to act on it. All of us have experienced the pain that comes from having to choose between two alternatives that appear equally inviting or equally repelling. I recall a trip which I made with my parents and my brothers when I was a youngster. On the trip, we stopped at my aunt's and uncle's home. The next morning at breakfast they had a beautiful assortment of French pastry. We never had anything like that at our home, and for some reason I was offered the first choice. But I couldn't choose. To take one was to leave the remainder! I vacillated until finally my aunt took the plate and passed it around the table. I died a thousand deaths each time one of those beautiful things was taken. I got the last pastry on the plate.

Because of constancy of perception, the perceptual field of a person at any one time resembles its structure at any other time. The choices we make reflect a consistency that makes each of us unique. This uniqueness is called personality. Personalities are the unique responses people make to the choices presented by the structure of their perceptual fields. This consistency in people's behavior helps us to understand them and predict their behavior. The consistency gives each of them their individuality.

The drive to maintain or enhance self-organization says that when we act on our environments, our behavior can be at one of two levels. At the first level, behavior maintains our status. At the second level, we seek to enhance that status. Whenever possible, we choose enhancement over maintenance. Enhancement of course is judged solely by the perceiver. Another person might judge a particular behavior as not adding to stature or debasing instead of enhancing. But it is the opinion of the behaver which counts. When other people react negatively to our behavior, we may regret our action and seek to change it. But the change is made as a result of the different perception we have of ourselves after our initial action. When we regret an action, it is because our field now contains our perception of what happened as a result of our initial behavior.

The behavior of delinquent children illustrates that the behaver's point of view is decisive in determining if behavior is enhancing or debasing. Delinquents, for example, sometimes want to be caught in criminal acts for the "status" they believe it gives them in the eyes of their peers. Nondelinquent children do not believe that criminal behavior enhances their self-organization. If delinquents ask when apprehended, "Will we get our pictures in the paper?" their opinions are clear. Students often say and do things in school which they believe will enhance them in the eyes of their peers and in spite of possible punishment. The pain of punishment is weighed against the possibility of enhancement.

Much student behavior is directed toward maintaining self-organization. When students behave to avoid failure, punishment, embarrassment, censure, or ridicule, they are seeking only to maintain self-organization. Students also engage in maintenance behavior when they do not see meaning in what is being learned. Even though what is supposed to be learned is meaningful to teachers, it does not have meaning for students until they see its personal relevance. Until then, students will react with maintenance behavior if they react at all. A fundamental problem for teachers is, "How can we help students find meaning in those things they must learn for survival?" If something is really needed for survival, it is usually not difficult to do this.

Sometimes, though, students learn because they believe that what they are learning is important and worthwhile. When this occurs, learning is a means of enhancing self-organization. If students are seeking only to maintain self-organization in school, they do not try very hard, and the chances of their discovering personal meaning in what is to be learned are minimal. If what is learned has little or no personal meaning or relevance, the chances of its being remembered are poor. The chances of its being used at a later date when it is needed are even less.

At the physiological level the same mechanism operates. When hungry, we eat to maintain ourselves. We drink water and breathe for the same purpose. When invaded by disease organisms, our bodies mobilize their defenses to restore their balance. In many instances, though, when our bodies defend themselves against disease they enhance their status by developing antibodies which help us to resist further attacks of the disease. Eating and drinking may also take on enhancement value; for example, when they are a part of "growing up" or part of a social process in adulthood.

Refraining from maintenance processes may also be enhancing. People diet to enhance their figures; fasts are helpful in attaining certain religious objectives; a child may hold its breath to achieve its ends. Social dissenters and prisoners sometimes seek reforms through hunger strikes. When maintenance processes are utilized in these ways, it is obvious that they are being used for purposes of enhancement.

What may appear to an observer to be self-destructive behavior may be a form of maintenance or even enhancement. For example, hara-kiri restores "lost face." The Kamikaze pilots of Japan in World War II loaded their planes with explosives and flew them into United States battleships. Dying in such an attempt was enhancing to self-organization, much like dying in battle was for the Vikings who joined Oden. Moslems who die in the defense of Islam go directly to heaven.

Suicide can be an attempt to maintain self-organization when its purpose is to avoid further destruction of the self. The person may believe, "If I keep on going, things will worsen and become intolerable." A person with a terminal illness may maintain self-organization through suicide.

The desire of people to grow and thus to enhance themselves is easily observed in young people. Infants often desire to perform more complex tasks than they are maturationally ready for. As infants mature, they want to do what their older brothers and sisters do. People believe that doing what other people are doing will make them more acceptable. If they are accepted by the people they value, they feel enhanced.

If students in school saw learning a new language as self-enhancing as they did learning their own language as infants, and if they spent as much time practicing the new language, the problem of foreign language instruction in schools would be solved. If learning a foreign language had as much personal meaning for students as learning their own language did, they would study it with as much enthusiasm. Students in a foreign country for example, learn the new language rapidly because it has personal meaning. The problem of language teachers is the same as the one that faces all teachers, "How can we help students discover personal meanings in what we are trying to teach them?" There is no simple answer.

Habit and Maintenance —

Maintenance of self-organization does not move the organism forward. It only helps it maintain its relative position. So the tendency of the organism is to carry out maintenance activities with a minimum of conscious effort. Eating, eliminating, sleeping, bathing, brushing one's teeth, and dressing become habitual. So do many other processes which serve to maintain self-organization. From the viewpoint of perceptual psychology, these processes become habitual as a result of their maintenance value and not from repetition as suggested by behavioristic psychologists. If and when their value in maintaining the physical self ceases, they disappear. The words "routinized" or "mechanized" describe maintenance behavior frequently performed better than does the word "habit." Whenever possible we make maintenance behavior as automatic as possible.

Maintenance behavior is not habit in the sense that it is done because we have become accustomed to doing it. Educators and parents who idealize controlling role concepts believe that scholarly habits and responsibility are developed through practice. They believe that when such behavior is practiced for a long enough period of time, students become "habituated" and will continue to do them after they are no longer required to do so. This explanation does not fit the facts from a perceptual point of view.

For example, about the time that infants comfortably adopt (have developed a "habit" of) a six-meal-a-day feeding schedule, they no longer have need for it. The infants' intake capacity has increased and they sleep more deeply for longer periods of time. When their need for a 2:00 a.m. feeding is gone, they no longer awaken to demand it. And when they have matured more fully, they no longer need five meals a day, whereupon they no longer demand five meals a day. Clearly, the number of feedings demanded by an infant is regulated by need and not by repetition or "habit." According to Skinner's theory, infants should continue to demand more and more feedings if they are on demand-feeding schedules, since on such schedules they are reinforced each time they demand to be fed. If Skinnerian psychologists use the fact that the infant is fed to satiation as an explanation for its changed "habits," we can point out that, conversely, most of the work done from Skinner's frame of reference has been done by denying satiation. This belies the general applicability of Skinner's principles.

When infants have learned that their hunger will be satisfied and also that they can communicate in ways other than crying, they no longer cry for food. When the need disappears, the habit disappears. If this did not happen, adults would cry for their dinners.

Self-Realization —

Habits help us fill maintenance needs with minimal effort. This frees us to behave in ways that will enhance our self-organization. How do we know what is enhancing to self-organization?

Enhancing experiences are those which move us toward *self-realization*, that is, toward becoming more experienced and discovering who we are in the meanings we discover in our present and past experiences. Without experience we are nothing. The meanings we perceive in our experience define us in our own eyes.

The human organism is *self-actualizing*, that is, capable of initiating action. The direction of that action, whenever possible, is toward self-realization and discovering one's self in new experience. People are not passively dependent on outside stimuli for starting them toward self-realization. Actually we do not respond directly to stimuli. Before we respond, a stimulus must enter our perceptual field and alter its structure. It is the altered field to which we respond.

The Structure of the Perceptual Field

The perceptual field is kaleidoscopic; and it is never the same in the instant following behavior as it was before the behavior. Indeed, it cannot be, since behavior usually results in feedback to the behaver and these new perceptions alter the structure of the field. Have you ever wished you could "bite off your tongue" as soon as you said something? Each of us have heard other people say something derogatory about another person. Their behavior has a different meaning for them if they realize they are overheard by the person about whom they were talking. As another example, when people do something for a prank and someone is injured, they no longer see what they did as prankish.

The perceptual field is also stable. It has a quality of constancy. Although the field is ever-changing, it also tends to remain the same. What we believe to be true today we probably will believe tomorrow. Our first learnings take priority over later ones and often interfere with new learning. When we have learned something, it is more difficult to learn something opposed to it than if we had never known anything about it.

Constancy of perception accounts for the fact that people seldom change their choice of political party or religious faith, and almost always feel positively toward their alma mater. It also accounts for many far less easily observable facts about people and for personality. Think of the problems we would encounter if each day we had an entirely different picture of our world and each day we again had to learn how to act upon it.

We receive communications through our sense organs: sight, smell, hearing, taste, touch, and others. Interaction with the environment stimulates these sense organs, giving rise to organic sensations. These sensations are the raw materials of experience — there is no other means by which we can experience. Overstimulation of any of the sense organs produces pain, and we attempt to withdraw from the noxious stimulus.

Infants are aware of the status of their organization and respond to stimuli which threaten the balance of that status. Their reactions are usually immediate and total. This means that infants are open to the meanings of their experience for their organisms. All new experience is evaluated in terms of its organic meanings. Thus infants are able to exercise judgment in regard to their needs, and they act in ways consistent with those needs even though the choices may not be conscious. When infants are hungry, they cry. When they are tired, they sleep. When they are uncomfortable, they react. When they need oxygen, they breathe. And when invaded by infectious diseases, they mobilize their defenses. But infants' sensitivity to their needs may extend far beyond this. For example, infants can select an adequate, well-balanced diet if the ingredients are available, and they can determine how much of this diet they need. When infants are hungry, they readily accept milk; when satiated, they just as readily reject it. They have an inborn valuing mechanism, their organism.

As infants interact with their environment, they receive stimuli which are interpreted in terms of their meanings for their organism. For a very young infant, there is a direct correspondence between sensation and perception. The meanings the infant attaches to his sensations to form his perceptions are those of his own organism.

Openness to Experience

How wonderful it would be if people could develop completely in tune with the organic meanings of their experience! Older children and adults, like infants, would be open to the meanings of their experience and would respond in terms of its personal meanings. Such completely open people would be as intelligent in their behavior as their experience would permit them to be. Intelligence would be limited only by lack of experience. The exception would be people with damaged or malfunctioning nervous systems which place limits on their ability to receive experience and its meanings. For most people, the quality of their behavior is limited by lack of experience *and* by lack of openness to its personal meanings.

As infants mature, they usually are taught to distrust or to deny many of their personal meanings. As toddlers children may, to satisfy curiosity, pick up an attractive object only to be told, "No." If they infer that picking it up is a "bad" thing, "bad" may be associated with curiosity or with wanting to learn. Too, they may conclude that curiosity can lead to punishment. Children may do something which gives themselves pleasure only to be told, "Nice people don't do things like that!" Children fall and hurt themselves, and some adult says that they are not really hurt. If a boy cries, he is called a baby. He discovers that to be acceptable, he must act as if someone else's beliefs are more valid than his own experience. He begins to deny or to distort his experience and its meanings. Whose experience is a child to trust?

Children trust their own experiencing until they are told by important people that their meanings are incorrect and are punished for those things which bring them pleasure. They like certain people or things until told by adults and other children that they are stupid or blind for doing so. Other people urge and sometimes force children to substitute their meanings for the children's. A person on whom a child depends for existence may threaten to withhold love to force him to accept their personal meanings. Consequently, as they mature, young people grow further and further from the meanings of their own experiencing.

We live in an evaluative world in which other people continuously try to substitute their meanings for ours. Instead of trying to understand us, they attempt to make us experience as they think we should. Carl Rogers expresses this clearly when he says:

*I have found it of enormous value when I can permit myself to understand another person. The way in which I have worded this statement may seem strange to you. Is it necessary to **permit** oneself to understand another? I think it is. Our first reaction to most of the statements we hear from other people is an immediate evaluation, or*

judgment, rather than an understanding of it. When someone expresses
some feeling or attitude or belief, our tendency is, almost immediately, to
feel 'That's right'; or 'That's stupid'; 'That's abnormal'; 'That's
unreasonable'; 'That's incorrect'; 'That's not nice.' Very rarely do we
permit ourselves to **understand** *precisely what the meaning of the*
statement is to him. I believe this is because understanding is risky. If I
let myself really understand another person, I might be changed by that
understanding. And we all fear change. So as I say, it is not an easy
thing to permit oneself to understand an individual, to enter thoroughly
and completely and empathically into his frame of reference. It is also a
rare thing [3].

Perceptions and Threat

When an event is perceived as potentially damaging, it is experienced as threatening. The possible damage may be either to the organism or to its state of organization. Potential physical injury is threatening, but it often is less threatening than the potential damage to or destruction of the self-concept.

The self-concept is the central aspect of our perceptual fields. It is the "picture" we have of ourselves, developed from our experience. Each significant experience — that is, each experience with personal meaning — contributes to this self-picture. Hopefully, each experience is perceived by a person in terms of its true meaning for his or her organism. If we have available the meanings of our experience without distortion or denial, there is a perfect correspondence between our self-concepts and our experiencing, and we *are* our experiencing. (Such an ideal condition probably never exists completely.)

The importance of the self-concept cannot be overemphasized. Although only a concept, to each of us it is real. It is us. Since the self-concept is central to our personalities, it is not surprising to discover that our most important perceptions are organized around it. It is because self-concept is so important that measures of it were included in the battery of instruments used to collect the data base discussed earlier [1]. These data show that the longer students continue in school, the more negative become their perceptions of themselves and other people. Thus the present direction of growth for many students is toward acting less intelligently, and therefore being less intelligent.

What we perceive is as consistent with our self-concept as we can make it. New perceptions which are inconsistent with our self-concept are denied or distorted to maintain consistency. Thus a person can have two conflicting meanings for experience — the true meaning for the organism and the meaning which appears in awareness. In cases of conflict, the self-concept emerges the victor. A separation occurs between experience and perception, and the person becomes less open to experience.

People's behavior is consistent with their concepts of themselves. Such behavior frequently serves to reinforce their self-concept. Students who believe they are poor spellers spell poorly, which proves to them that they are poor spellers. Thus the self-concept is both a result and a cause. It results from the abstracting of experiencing, but it also determines what experience will be abstracted and how future experience will be interpreted. People who perceive themselves as inadequate, inferior, disliked, unattractive, and so forth select experiences which reinforce their self-concept and interpret new experience in ways consistent with their self-concept.

The strongest threats that people feel are threats to their self-concept. Anything which is perceived as potentially damaging to the self-concept or which requires or forces a change in it is seen as threatening. Under threat people defend themselves. They do this by narrowing or restricting their perceptual field, distorting the meaning of experience, denying experience, or all of these. People who are defending themselves may fail "to see the facts" so they can defend themselves, or they may not symbolize experience into awareness, or their awareness of an experience may be different from its meanings for their organisms. Abnormal psychology is a study of behavior under conditions of threat. Under threat a person becomes less open to experience and its meanings. When this happens, the person's intelligence is reduced.

Threat occurs primarily when damage to self-concept appears imminent, and when its principal source is people who are important to us. These may be our parents, teachers, peers, or other people. The greatest threats these people pose are their disapproval or withholding of love. When we fear that important people will disapprove of us or that they will love us less, we distort and deny the meanings of our experience so that we can behave as they demand. As a consequence we have an inadequate basis for behaving, and we learn to distrust our own experiencing. The locus of our self-evaluation is centered outside ourselves, and we are motivated more by the desires of important other people than by our own organismic meanings. We attempt to behave on the basis of someone else's perceptions, not our own. When we do this, we are psychologically "sick." Our intelligence is diminished.

When we are threatened, we attempt to reject the threat. We may attack the threatening object or person in an effort to destroy it. Or we can reject the threat by selective perception, denial of experience, or distorting its meaning. Consequently, people under threat are in a process of rejecting their experience and its meanings, usually with negative affective responses. The negative attitudes of people who are closed to their experiencing may be directed toward themselves, other people, institutions, or anything which poses a threat. Thus attitude helps assess the presence or absence of threat. For this reason, measures of students' attitudes toward themselves, other people, and school were included in the data base [1] along with measures of their parents' attitudes toward the schools. These data show that the longer students remain in school, the more negative their attitudes and those of their parents become. Thus students are less able to profit from schooling than they might be. The development of their intelligence suffers.

These generalizations about how people react to threat were illustrated earlier by teachers' perceptions of their problems. Teachers who describe their most pressing concerns as something like "teaching boys and girls who have neither the desire nor the ability to learn" are expressing negative attitudes toward students. They perceive the problem as outside themselves, which means that they do not have to change. These perceptions help them manage the threatening perception that students are not learning as their teachers believe they should.

Teachers who describe their most pressing problem as something like "discovering newer and better ways of helping children learn" are seeking to incorporate new experience and to change. Their attitudes toward the children are positive; they see themselves as responsible for changing; they feel capable of changing; and they are accepting of the fact that they must continue to change in order to become more helpful. Thus teachers' problems offer a means of assessing their openness to experience.

Threat and Helping Relationships

We live in a world characterized by the threat of evaluation from people who are important to us. Our relationships with other people are evaluative rather than accepting. People seldom accept our behavior without evaluation, and even less frequently help us to assess our own behavior.

At times the evaluation a child receives is positive rather than negative. But even positive evaluation is threatening, forcing the locus of responsibility to become external. When other people evaluate us positively, they imply that they have a right to evaluate. This in turn implies that negative evaluations of our behavior will be forthcoming if they do not approve. Thus positive evaluation may create defensive behavior in much the same way as negative evaluation, and we become less open to experience.

Fortunately, the process of defending oneself against threat and becoming more closed to experiencing is reversible, that is, if the threats are removed and the amount of defensive behavior is not too severe. Although the greatest potential threats are those which come from people important to us, the same people can be our greatest source of help in becoming more open to our experiencing. Several sources of evidence, including the data base [1], show that under favorable classroom conditions, positive personality change can occur which may be as great as that which can result from individual counseling. Very defensive people — those who believe they have greater worth than other people (+ -) — do not often profit from individual counseling. They may, however, be aided in classrooms.

If important other people evaluate or reject us, we are threatened and become more defensive, denying and distorting experience and its personal meanings. If, though, important other people accept us as worthwhile and permit use to be our experience, the basic drive to enhance self-organization is free to operate. We become more open to the meanings of our experience; we become more experienced; we become our experience; and we become more intelligent.

The characteristics of a helping relationship have already been described (page 78). A relationship is helpful if the helping person has an unconditional, positive regard for the people being helped and if the helper is empathic and congruent. Such a relationship is relatively threat-free for the people being helped. If they perceive the relationship as low in threat, the drive toward enhancement of self-organization can operate and they can move toward becoming their experience.

Because of prior experiences, some people receiving help do not immediately perceive the threat-free nature of a helping relationship. They assume that it is similar to other relationships they have had with important other people. If, though, the helping person provides the relationship consistently and over a long enough period of time, only the most seriously disturbed people do not move toward becoming their experience.

When people are their experience, they are able to base their behavior on all of their experience. They can receive new experience continuously and in terms of its meaning for their organism. Consequently, the quality of their behavior is superior to what it would be if they were less open to their experience. *They behave more intelligently, which means that they are more intelligent.*

Measure of the four helping relationship characteristics are included in the data base [1]. These measures show that in the average school relationships with teachers, as seen by students, are not as helpful as they might be. As a consequence, students develop negative feelings about their school and see their teachers as dominating them. If schools are to help students become more intelligent, teachers must provide more helpful relationships.

References

1. Bills, R. E. Summary Data and Interpretations: A System for Assessing Affectivity. *ERIC* ED 166 243.
2. Combs, A. W., Richards, A. C. and Richards, F. *Perceptual Psychology.* New York: Harper and Row, 1976.
3. Rogers, C. R. *On Becoming a Person.* Boston: Houghton-Mifflin, 1961.

Chapter Thirteen

The Implications:

What Students Need for the Development of Their Intelligence

Perceptual theory has numerous implications for teaching. As a whole, these implications describe the qualities of educational experiences students need for the development of intelligence.

Implication 1

To teach people, we must understand them; and this is most easily accomplished by trying to see them and their worlds as they see themselves.

What people do is in agreement with reality as it appears to them at the instant of action. Not what is true but what they believe to be true governs their actions. Attempts to dissuade them may increase their defensiveness and strengthen their convictions. We can understand their behavior only if see the world as they see it. If we wish to be helpful, we must accept the world as they see it and not attempt to coerce or to seduce them into changing.

Obviously, this position disagrees with other methods of trying to change people. Many people believe that teachers should decide what students should be like, then arrange students' experiences so they must change. The morality of this way of changing people within our society must be questioned. Worse still, the data presented in this book show that when schools assume the right to mold students in the ideal adults hold for them, the results are often harmful to students. Their intelligence is reduced.

Understanding students is not the difficult task it has been made out. It is not necessary to "do" something specific to each individual student to communicate to all students. We know that if a teacher treats one student unfairly, this unfairness is felt by all of the students. Conversely, if a teacher shows fairness to one student, it raises the expectations of all of the students that they will be treated fairly.

Understanding does not have to be "deep" in a psychological sense to have meaning for people. Teachers can communicate understanding in a thousand ways, none of which require much effort or time — a warm smile to a child the first time they meet each day; a comment to a smiling youngster, "You look happy;" a touch on a student's shoulder as the teacher goes by; a simple statement like "You look disappointed" to a child who obviously is feeling this way; a comment that shows that the teacher understands the pleasure a child is experiencing from a task well-done; the recognition that a task is difficult or boring. All these and many other simple actions show that teachers are interested and concerned, and that the student is an important person. When teachers do this to one student, they do it to all of them. They also create a climate in which intelligence can develop.

Implication 2

Our first learnings take precedence over later ones.

The first attitudes students hold toward people, institutions, school subjects, and other things may be the ones that they retain for the remainder of their lives. If so, their behavior will reflect any inadequacy in their generalizations, and as a result they will be less intelligent. New experiences help students modify their concepts; but when they become defensive, they do not change. Adequate learning or relearning is aided by reducing their defensiveness. This means that schools must do what they can to prevent students from becoming defensive and reduce whatever defensiveness they have.

Subject-matter should be presented under the most favorable attitudinal conditions, for example, when students are ready to learn and when they see the value of it for them. If students feel threatened, they develop negative attitudes which become associated with what is being learned and prevent meaningful learning.

Implication 3

Consistency of perception is a fundamental characteristic of people and must be considered in any educational program.

Consistency of perception has value in helping us to adjust to our kaleidoscopic perceptual fields. In a world in which things seldom appear twice in the same context, the ability to maintain perceptual constancy has untold value. In an educational setting, consistency can also be a handicap. The purpose of education can be achieved only when students change their perceptions. This means that schools must do what they can to optimize the possibility of students changing. Optimal conditions include interactive decision-making with teachers who are seen as unconditionally positive in their regard, and empathic, and congruent. The data show that these conditions do not exist in the schools, and the further students go in school, the less optimal the conditions are.

A major deterrent to developing optimal school climates is the belief that the sole purpose of schools is to develop informed people. It is assumed that this purpose can be achieved when well-informed teachers communicate their knowledge to students. This concept of teaching reduces the effectiveness of teachers. Their relationships with students suffer; students become defensive and protect themselves against change; students develop negative self-concepts, negative attitudes toward other people, and negative attitudes toward their schools; students have fewer opportunities to make decisions for themselves and to influence what is happening to them. As a consequence, students defend themselves against change. They do not develop their intelligence as they might.

Implication 4

Education must start with the problems of people.

Perceptions which significantly influence behavior develop in situations that are meaningful and offer promise for enhancement of self-organization. In school, though, learning usually starts with problems teachers believe are important. Such problems are usually aimed at students' future needs. This leads to difficulty since students often do not see these as meaningful. Snygg and Combs [1] state that problem behavior in schools most often results from teachers attempting to teach for future need fulfillment to students who are in need of immediate need satisfaction.

When schools start teaching problems such as number combinations because they will be needed by students some time in the future, they divorce the learning from the purposes and needs of the learners. Unless teaching starts where the learners are, the learning is meaningless. Teachers must help students see that number combinations are important for solving what students believe are meaningful problems.

The data discussed in this book show that students have insufficient opportunity to interact with their teachers in classroom decision-making. The longer students remain in school, the less opportunity they have to influence what they will study, so it becomes less likely that what they study will have personal meaning for them. Again, the results negatively affect the development of intelligence.

Implication 5

Since needs, values, and attitudes are important parts of meaning and determiners of perceptions, education must seek to help students know what needs, values, and attitudes are important to them, and to consider these fully and in relation to each other.

Controlling teachers attempt to teach students what the teachers think they need, what they should value, and how they should feel about important things. Facilitating teachers help students discover personal meanings in past and new experience. There is no assurance that what students are taught by controlling teachers will be meaningful. Yet my studies and those of my students show that the longer students remain in school, the more likely they will be taught by controlling teachers.

Elementary teachers idealize facilitating roles; teachers in departmentalized schools and in secondary schools idealize controlling roles. Thus in elementary schools, students have more opportunity to interact with their teachers and to explore meanings. It is little wonder that facilitating teachers are rated as more successful by their principals. Such teachers help students develop their intelligence.

Facilitating teachers, in comparison with controlling teachers, are seen by their students as more interactive. They are seen as providing relationships characterized by higher levels of positive and unconditional regard, empathic understanding and congruence. In such relationships, threat is minimal as is the need to defend oneself against change. Students can explore and discover personal meanings in experience. Facilitating teaching roles help students discover their needs, values, and attitudes, and the personal meanings of their experience. In this way, teachers help students become more intelligent.

Implication 6

Personal perceptions are not readily changed through the introduction of objective evidence.

People change when they discover personal meaning in their experience. Presenting them with objective evidence does not mean that they will find it personally meaningful and will change as a consequence. If other people attempt to force them to change by presenting them with objective evidence, they may find it threatening. When threatened, people deny and distort experience. They do not find it personally meaningful and they are not changed by it.

When people examine objective evidence and find it personally meaningful, they are changed by it. Interactive teachers, assisting students in such explorations, are seen by them as more helpful than teachers who make important decisions for students. This emphasizes what has already been said, that the types of decision-making and interpersonal relationships existing in our schools do not assist students in changing. Often relationships threaten students and cause them to defend themselves. As a result, they frequently do not find school experiences meaningful, and they are denied opportunities to become more intelligent.

Implication 7

The learning of adequate perceptions of self and of other people is most easily accomplished in warm interaction with people.

The perceptions we have of ourselves and of other people develop in interaction with people. Changes in perceptions can result only from further interaction. Further interaction, though, may not be enough. The quality of change is directly related to the degree of threat present in the interaction.

Intelligent behavior requires adequate perceptions. To the degree that perceptions of experience match the organic meanings of the experience, perceptions are adequate. Personality is adequate to the degree that experience and its personal meanings can be admitted into awareness without distortion [2]. It follows, then, that adequacy of perceptions and personality are basic to intelligent behavior.

The qualities of interpersonal relationships provided by teachers determine the adequacy of the personalities of their students. Teachers who provide warm, nonthreatening interactions for their students help them develop adequate perceptions. Such teachers aid the development of intelligence. Again, our research findings indicate that teachers too infrequently provide such helpful relationships for their students.

Implication 8

People grow in the absence of threat.

Under threatening conditions people defend themselves. They do not grow. Their efforts are directed to maintaining self-organization, and overcoming or eliminating the threat. Also under threat their perceptual fields become distorted and constricted.

That which is learned under threat is rapidly forgotten when the threat is removed. Under threat of failure, students may seem to learn that for which they have no particular need and which they do not find relevant or meaningful. Overcoming the threat becomes need-satisfying because it enables them to maintain their self-organization. But when the threat is removed — when students have their final report cards or diplomas — they rapidly forget material which was not meaningful to them. Worse still, since they have not found schoollike learning meaningful, they will not continue to study and read to learn.

School is a threatening experience. As a consequence schools often fail to fulfill their missions. Some schools are more successful than others in providing climates in which threat is reduced and in which students can develop their intelligence. Teachers have it in their power to provide such climates, but they are often limited in doing so by their role concepts and the beliefs of parents and other influential adults. The pressures of parents and other adults are the greatest deterrent to providing climates in which children can become more intelligent.

Implication 9

Physiological factors are important determiners of perceptions, and schools must do what they can to help make them optimal.

Hungry, sick, tired, or poorly clothed children do not learn as they might. Schools recognize their responsibilities for these and other factors such as seating, lighting, and ventilation. Oftentimes, though, they have been forced to prove that things such as providing adequate meals are also necessary for physical health and thus essential to learning.

Schools cannot do everything for children. They can feed hungry children and they can teach about good health. But they cannot help children get the rest they need if they come to school too sleepy to learn. They cannot overcome the diet problems which many children have because their families do not provide nutritious diets for them. Parents let their children stay up so late at night and eat so poorly that it interferes with their learning. Still they expect the schools to be effective.

Implication 10

Opportunity for a variety of meaningful experience is necessary for the development of intelligence.

This implication relates to the content of instruction. Since this is what schools are most concerned with, we might suppose that this is what they do best. Beyond the elementary subjects of reading, writing, and arithmetic, though, there is little agreement about what the content of an education should be. There appears to be no adequate answer to the question, "What school subjects best educate students?"

Yet as this book has shown, schools must teach in ways that help students find personal meaning in what they are learning. If schools are seeking to develop intelligent students, they must provide opportunities for students to examine the values and attitudes inherent in what is being taught. This means that discussions of controversial issues must be encouraged. In the 1960s, England changed its compulsory school attendance law so that students had to attend until they were 16 years old rather than 14. After careful consideration, it was decided that the cirruculum of the last two years should consist of controversial issues taught by teachers especially trained to center students' concerns on the issues and their meanings, and to help them avoid conflicts in discussions. How sad that English schools wait until their children are 14 years old to discuss meaningful issues! How much sadder that even at 14, children in our schools do not have opportunity to examine such issues. The saddest thing is that controversial issues are not discussed at any grade level.

Discussions of controversial issues are of value in promoting adequate perceptions of self and others. Issues are controversial only if they are personally meaningful. Interactions of students in such meaningful discussions always involve their values, attitudes, self-concepts, and concepts of other people. It is within the context of meaningful discussions held in warm, accepting, and non-evaluative environments that all of the factors necessary for the development of intelligence can be fostered.

Implication 11

Education must start where children are and permit them to determine their own directions and pace.

Teachers have no choice but to start where the learners are and let them determine the direction and pace of their learning, if their education is to be meaningful and if it is to develop intelligence. As much as teachers might like to start somewhere else, learners can only begin where they are.

Even though these statements may seem self-evident, they are continuously violated in the schools. Although students in a classroom differ significantly from each other in their understanding of a subject, most teachers start at the same point in instructing them. Teachers assume that all students are alike. Even if all students were alike at the beginning of a course, they would not stay this way since some learn faster than others. These differences in initial readiness and learning speed are usually overlooked since teachers do not see any alternative. "Standards" and curricular demands cause teachers to believe that they must "cover" the specified amount of material so that students will be prepared for the next course or the next grade. What happens, of course, is that the students who learn most rapidly learn the material and the remainder fall further and further behind.

The solution lies in working with students so that they become responsible for their own learning. Students must learn how to design their own courses of study. Teaching by means of student "contracts" in effect in many schools has demonstrated the feasibility of such a plan.

The notion that students should plan for themselves with assistance from their teachers may sound radical. It would be if we were to put it into effect immediately at all grade levels.

Students would be overwhelmed by the responsibility. Such a plan must be introduced gradually beginning in the first grade; first grade teachers must give students even more responsibility for their learning than they do at present. The abrupt break between grades 4 and 5 or 5 and 6 which presently occurs must be abolished.

One idea recommended for consideration is the tutorial system practiced in the best private schools in this country and Europe for many years. This, of course, demands that public school class size be reduced and the availability of resource materials increased. It also requires that we do away with the lock step curriculum, and even with grouping children by grades and promoting them from one grade to another. Grades were created for the convenience of schools, not because they had anything to do with how students learn.

Even if we cannot initiate these innovative procedures, we can maximize teachers' concerns for creating learning climates in which each student is free to explore meanings, values, attitudes, and self-concepts. One of the most important findings of the surveys described in this book is that schools differ markedly from each other in the quality of the experience they offer students. Some schools have students with positive attitudes toward their schools. These students describe their teachers as interactive and as offering them helping relationships. In other schools which appear equivalent in size and socio-economic levels, the findings are negative. The first kind of school is helping students develop their intelligence. The second kind offers little assistance. The difference is in the quality of leadership the teachers are afforded and in the openness of the teachers to their experience.

References

1. Snygg, D. and Combs, A. W. *Individual Behavior.* New York: Harper, 1949.
2. Combs, A. W., Richards, A. C. and Richards, F. *Perceptual Psychology.* New York: Harper and Row, 1976.

Chapter Fourteen

Five Major Recommendations:

How They Can Be Implemented in Today's Education System

A goodly number of recommendations has already been made, but some important considerations remain. These are described below along with recommendations for addressing them.

Some General Considerations

Changes in education have increased the psychological distance between parents and teachers and between teachers and students. Thirty or forty years ago, most elementary school pupils were taught in self-contained classrooms. Today many are taught in departmentalized classrooms by teachers responsible for 120 to 150 or more students each day. Teachers meet so many students in their departmentalized classrooms that they cannot possibly know them as individual people. It is also impossible for teachers to maintain adequate communication with parents, many of whom are employed and unavailable for conferences.

The problems schools encounter are multiplied by their differential effects on the attitudes of boys and girls, black and white students, rich and poor students, and others. The range of individual differences in any of these groups presents difficult problems for teachers in understanding their students as individual people. The large, heterogeneous groups of students presented to most teachers in departmentalized classrooms make understanding impossible.

Teachers' problems are magnified further by the functioning levels of students. Some students seek only to maintain themselves in school. Others seek to enhance themselves through their school experiences. Some find school boring, others find it exciting. Furthermore, all young people do not desire the same things from school. What is relevant for one youngster may not be for another. All of these factors must be considered if teaching is to be effective. Each teacher must have as small a number of *different* youngsters to react to as possible, and as great an amount of time as possible in which to react. Departmentalized instruction is the poorest means of assuring these two requirements; self-contained classrooms are superior.

Teachers differ in the roles they idealize. Facilitating teachers are more helpful in developing intelligent behavior in students than are controlling teachers. The school curriculum and organization, though, make it easier for teachers to practice a controlling role than a facilitating one. So what many people believe constitutes a good education defeats teachers' efforts to achieve more positive goals in their teaching.

One consequence of controlling role concepts is that students come to view schooling as an enterprise in which teachers and textbooks act on them. They conclude that they are expected to act passively and to assimilate facts, generalizations, and so forth which have little or no personal meaning for them. Thus school is oppressive. It increases in oppressiveness from grade to grade as the subject-matter becomes less and less personally relevant.

Large schools are more impersonal and more oppressive than small ones because the psychological distance between teachers and students is greater. For the same reason, relationships of students and teachers deteriorate with increases in grade since more departmentalized instruction is encountered.

School organization is also a complicating factor. Schools should be organized in ways which enable teachers to teach most effectively. Organization should not dictate teachers' roles. It should permit them maximum opportunity to teach in a manner consistent with their ideals, and to shift methods according to their goals. The departmentalized school is an efficient organization for controlling teachers. It is a poor plan for facilitating teachers. In self-contained classrooms, however, teachers can be either facilitating or controlling. Teachers in self-contained elementary school classrooms can practice controlling roles when they are teaching arithmetic fundamentals or spelling, if they think this is best; and they can practice facilitating roles when they are teaching more open-ended subjects such as reading and science.

Differences in teachers' and students' socio-economic backgrounds demand opportunities for the exercise of a variety of teaching roles. Students who expect teachers to be authoritarian, like other adults they have experienced, must have different relationships with their teachers than those who have experienced more interactive and democratic relationships with adults. For the former, a highly interactive teacher may be seen as "soft"; for the latter, even an interactive teacher may be seen as a dictator. Yet these children must be taught in the same classroom at the same time. Classroom organization must permit the operation of a variety of teacher-student relationships.

Teachers must also have leeway to practice roles consistent with their perceptions of what students need. Teachers must start where they are and with the children as they are. They must have freedom to move toward more effective roles as they and the children can profit from them. The form of organization of a school should not dictate the practice of teaching roles. These should be dictated by the experiential meanings of the people most affected by them — the students and the teachers.

Differences in instructional goals and techniques are dictated, also, by the functioning levels of the students. If students are functioning to maintain self-organization, teachers are wise to teach for this level. When the students are ready to move forward, teaching for enhancement is appropriate. If students are functioning to maintain self-organization, they probably can profit more from controlling teachers. If, though, the students are seeking enhancement of self-organization, controlling teachers will stifle their progress; they need facilitating teachers. It is for reasons such as these that schools should not have to teach children who are seeking to maintain self-organization in the same classrooms with those seeking to enhance self-organization. When they seek different levels of functioning, they probably should be taught in separate classrooms. Schools, however, do not have the option of doing this except in neighborhood schools, where students tend to form homogeneous groups.

If students are to learn to accept responsibility for themselves, schools must be organized to maximize their opportunities for close interpersonal relationships with warmly regarding teachers. This is essential at all levels and particularly in elementary schools. It takes time and opportunity for teachers to develop this kind of relationship with students. Few teachers can do it in 50-minute periods in which the emphasis is on cognitive learning. It is easier to do in self-contained classrooms where teachers are in contact with the same students during most of the school day.

Some students function at or below the level of maintenance of self-organization. Severely retarded children who are unable to care for themselves function below the level of maintenance of self-organization. You need only observe their satisfaction when they learn simple acts such as tying their own shoes or feeding or dressing themselves to conclude that such learnings are highly desirable. Behavior modification has made it possible to teach this kind of behavior to some children who otherwise would never have learned it.

There are children in the public schools who function at only slightly higher levels than the children just described. Learning goals for these children, like those for children in schools for the retarded, should be formulated to help them maintain themselves. Retarded learners are not being deprived of opportunities to be responsible for themselves when operant conditioning principles are applied. Instead, their ability to exercise responsibility is enhanced.

But what about children above the maintenance level? In general, such children should not be deprived of opportunities to be responsible for themselves and become increasingly responsible. There are exceptions. People who complete school unable to read at a sixth grade level, without command of the fundamental arithmetic processes, and unable to communicate in writing can maintain themselves only with difficulty and frequently become public responsibilities. When students complete school lacking competence in the three R's, both they and society suffer. There is justification to use whatever methods are available, including operant conditioning, to help them learn what it is that all of us know they must learn. If they cannot find personal meaning when they are taught by methods which help them accept responsibility for themselves, and if teachers have tried these methods for a long enough period of time to become convinced that they will not find personal meaning and learn by them, behavior modification should be applied. We owe it to these children. The large majority of students, though, learn by less restrictive methods. They should not be taught by any method which reduces their opportunities for being responsible for themselves.

A final consideration can be raised in the form of a question, "Do all children need a high school education?" What relevance does high school, as currently organized and as its subjects are currently taught, have for the lives of non-college-bound students? Those students who like school or particular subjects and those who believe they must succeed in high school to succeed in college are fortunate. They see some meaning in their high school studies. So, too, do the small number of students in distributive education, vocational education, and business courses who plan careers in these fields. And some of the promising athletes who aspire to college and professional sports careers may also see their needs being satisfied. Unfortunately only those students who plan college careers are valued by most teachers.

For many students, high schools offer little that is need-relevant. These students attend as long as the laws compel attendance, or long enough to get diplomas because without them too many doors are closed. How few of these "doors" really require a high school education even though high school graduation is generally a requirement! We have fallen into a trap. Before such a large percentage of students completed high school, those who graduated showed superior intelligence to those who dropped out. High school graduation became a screening process acceptable to business and industry. Today, because people must have high school diplomas to be employed in many jobs, the diploma is no longer an effective screening device for employment although it is still a requirement.

There are those who deplore the fact that high school graduation today does not insure that the graduate is a superior person. Such people believe that schools owe it to society to graduate certifiable people and serve as screening agencies for employment needs. This is not the school's purpose. The responsibility of schools is to the students and not to industry or business. Schools cannot serve two masters. They were created to help students learn those things they need in order to behave intelligently. They were not created to save the nation or to insure high-caliber employees for business and industry. When schools began to teach need-irrelevant subjects, they began to take on the role of certifying agent to force students to learn things that were not intrinsically meaningful. Schools which deny students diplomas often deny them opportunity to be hired in jobs for which they are competent. This is a dilemma. If schools maintain their standards, they deny students employment. High school curricula need to be modified to be more meaningful, and standards of competence must be demanded long before high school graduation.

Five General Recommendations

The foregoing discussion along with discussion in previous chapters leads to five general recommendations. The recommendations are simple. They can be carried out in most school districts with little change in current methods of operation and with no increase in cost. Actually, these recommendations, if implemented, can save money although this is not their purpose.

Recommendation I. The first recommendation is that the qualities of decision-making and interpersonal relationships between students and their teachers must be improved. Unless they are, schools cannot hope to help students find meaning in their educational experiences and develop their intelligence to the degree they should. Inadequate interpersonal relationships are causing many children to behave less intelligently than they should. Adequate relationships with teachers and a greater voice in decision-making processes for students can help to reduce the rate of violence and vandalism in the schools, the juvenile crime rate, and the use of alcohol and drugs which are now appearing in problem proportions in middle schools.

What would it cost to treat our children as responsible and worthwhile people? It would not cost schools anything. Not so obvious is how schools can reverse the process they are now engaged in. The first step is to reorganize priorities. What is more important, children or subject-matter? Subject-matter is important only when students perceive it as meaningful. When subject-matter is not need-relevant, it becomes oppressive and those connected with it are seen as oppressors.

Evidence shows that the psychological climate of a school is in large part determined by its principal. To the degree that a principal can offer teachers a helping relationship, to that same degree the teachers can grow in openness and offer the students helping relationships. When principals are arbitrary and autocratic, teachers gripe and complain instead of trying to change and improve.

It is not easy for principals to provide such a climate, especially when they are subject to pressures from superintendents and parents. But to the degree that a principal can provide a faculty with a helping relationship in which its members can become more open to experience, to the same degree the faculty members will reciprocate and provide a helping relationship for the principal as well as students. People create their own climate for change. People who help other people in turn are helped. This principle operates in industry, business, homes, and elsewhere.

One of the greatest deterrents to principals providing leadership and helping relationships for teachers is the current corporate model of management adopted by school administrators. It is easier to manage than to lead, and it has more prestige. But it does not get the educational job done.

Even if principals do not, will not, or cannot provide helping relationships for faculty members, there is no excuse for faculty members not to attempt to improve classroom climates to the fullest possible extent. When teachers close their doors, they decide how to behave toward students. Teachers often say that they would like to change but they are not permitted to do so. However, principals, superintendents, and parents seldom complain about teachers as long as students are satisfied with what is going on in their classrooms.

Recommendation II. The second recommendation flows from the first one. The greatest barrier to adequate classroom relationships is the large number of students that teachers must teach each day when instruction is departmentalized. Departmentalization robs teachers of the necessary time for establishing adequate and warm working relationships with students. They cannot react adequately to the complex variables present in any classroom.

The problem of adjusting to a new group of students each 50 minutes is as overwhelming as the problem of adjusting to the wide range of individual differences present in any group. Extended periods of time are needed to establish the relationships that learners need to become more intelligent people.

The problem is further complicated by variables such as those discussed in this book. The wide range of individual student differences present in most classrooms creates threatening relationships for teachers. Teachers become less open to their experience and defend themselves. As a consequence, they cannot offer students the type of relationship the students need to become more open to their experience and more intelligent.

It has also been shown that teachers interact differently and have important differences in the quality of relationships with male and female students. And it has been shown by the research that male and female students, black and white students, rich and poor students are set to experience their teachers in different ways.

All of these factors influence the quality of teaching and learning. Teachers must have opportunities to experience students as individuals so they can attend to the qualities of their interactions and personal relationships. Students must also have sufficient exposure to teachers so that they can understand them and become less defensive in relationships with them.

The ideal situation for promoting such opportunities is a self-contained classroom. In it teachers can learn to know their students and students their teachers. The alternative to self-contained classrooms is homogeneous grouping of students and teachers — separate classes for girls and boys, black and white students, rich and poor students, male and female teachers, and black and white teachers. This would not solve the problem. It would only isolate people from each other and from opportunities to learn from each other.

Because of these and other reasons, it is recommended that students be taught in self-contained classrooms to the fullest degree possible. They should be taught in such settings through the eighth grade and in at least modified form beyond that point. Schools should return to an 8-4 plan of organization. If textbook-centered subject-matter instruction is retained in the high school grades, combinations of subjects should be taught back-to-back so that one teacher can have the same students more than one period. In this way, the number of individual students taught by one teacher would be halved. The most natural combinations for such teaching are English and social studies, science and mathematics. Other combinations can be formed such as bookkeeping and typewriting, and economics and business law. Too, combinations could be formed by teaching two years of a subject such as foreign language in one year by using double periods. Curriculum revision could make subjects more meaningful and capable of being taught in larger blocks of time.

Two major reasons have been given for departmentalizing instruction. First, it is believed that only well trained experts in a field can properly teach a subject. There is no disagreement with this contention. The most flexible instruction in a subject can be given only by teachers who know the subject well. Teachers who do not have full command of a subject must stick slavishly to the textbook and cannot permit students to explore more deeply. These teachers fear that students will get into areas in which they are not informed and thus they teach the textbook chapter by chapter.

It is not necessary for high school teachers to have the degree of competence in a subject-matter area, however, that is represented by a master's degree. A more appropriate use of their time in graduate programs would be to help them keep up with changes in their fields. Digging more deeply into the field will not assure greater competence for high school level teachers. More preparation usually means greater specialization. This does not assure greater knowledge of what is to be taught.

A second reason given for departmentalized instruction is that in self-contained classrooms some children are "stuck" for an entire year with a poor teacher. But the cure for poor teaching is not to departmentalize instruction. It is to help poor teachers improve or get rid of them. If schools reorganize without doing something about the teachers, poor teachers are still teaching students and are now teaching greater numbers of students. The reasoning that poor teachers will have contact with any one student for a shorter period of time is just an excuse. How long does it take some teachers to traumatize students? It is the responsibility of the teaching profession to rid itself of such people. It should not be necessary to reorganize schools to dilute their effects.

If the subject-matter which is being taught at the seventh and eighth grade levels is so complex that it requires specialists to teach it, then its relevance for most of the learners is questionable. Why should all learners have to suffer because some of them may need the information at a later date? The data presented in this book about what is happening to students should disabuse anyone of the notion that schools can continue to try to educate people as they currently are doing.

One other type of consideration enters into the recommendation that students be retained in self-contained classrooms as long as possible. In part, this relates to relationships among the children. One of the major sources of oppression which students, particularly boys, experience is physical aggression from other boys.

A second part of the consideration is what inexperienced

and immature people can do to themselves, such as, alcohol and drug abuse which are appearing with frightening frequency as low as grades 4 and 5. Teachers who have adequate opportunity to know their students know almost immediately that such things are occurring. The situation can be dealt with before it becomes serious. Today it is possible for students to sit quietly "stoned" in their classrooms without teachers being aware of it. More importantly, teachers in self-contained classrooms have opportunities to help youngsters examine their relationships with each other and make more responsible decisions for themselves than they can without guidance. At the same time that guidance from families has diminished, opportunities for guidance in classrooms has also decreased.

Closely related to the recommendation that children be taught in self-contained classrooms is the recommendation that elementary schools be as small as possible, preferably one class with 25 students per grade — 200 per school. In such a context teachers can become acquainted with all of the students in the school and help supervise all of them.

Recommendation III. The third recommendation concerns flexibility in the secondary school curriculum. The high school curriculum and high school courses must be as flexible and offer as much choice as possible. They should also deal with controversial materials.

The high school curriculum was inherited from its predecessors. The curricula of the academies and the Latin grammar schools were practical, intended for a select group of people who would use what they were taught in specific occupations or further professional preparation. Because some of the subjects have been taught for so long, it has been assumed that they have intrinsic value, and that all people need these courses for "cultural" or for other reasons. These courses were originally need-relevant but they became meaningless for many students as the holding power of schools increased.

A large proportion of high school students continues on into college. To the greatest degree possible, they need to be prepared for success in college. But this is not done through subject-matter alone. All college curricula do not require the same backgrounds. Actually, most elementary college courses assume that students have had no previous work in the field and start from scratch. Naturally students who have studied the subject previously have a head start. But it is not requisite and all students should not have to study a subject just because some will do further study in it. Self-discipline and success in whatever is studied are at least as important in college preparation as what is studied.

A frequently heard argument is that unless students are introduced to subjects such as chemistry, physics, mathematics, and the like, they will not know whether or not they should pursue them in college. That seems reasonable. But does it mean that the best way to help students learn about a field is to give them technical preparation in it? This is doubtful. It is probably more important for high school students to learn the methods of study used in a field, the structure of the discipline, and means of evaluating data and drawing conclusions within a discipline than it is to learn the "facts" of the subject. This is another way of saying that it is more important for high school students to learn *how* to think in a subject-matter field than to learn *what* to think.

When people hear something that does not agree with what they already believe, they usually ignore it or forget it. That is what happened to the findings of a very important study done in the 1940s at the University of Kentucky, the University of Cincinnati, and Indiana University. The study sought an answer to the question, "What courses or combinations of courses best prepare students for college?" The answer was, "None." Students at the three universities who entered a particular subject with a background in the subject were matched on academic ability with students who did not have the subject as background. Then their success in the college course was compared. Conversely, the success of students with similar high school backgrounds who entered different fields in college were compared. The study concluded that no one course of study best prepares students for college. Colleges should not require a particular background for any student. But colleges are acting appropriately when they require that whatever students do in high school be done with success. Few colleges today require specific courses for entrance, although most people believe they do.

Almost any subject can be the starting point for a technical or professional education. Students who want to be housepainters can be helped to master the technology. They need not stop there. By the time they have mastered the technology, they may have so many unanswered questions about pigments, vehicles, driers, thinners, and the like that they may be ready to study chemistry and become paint chemists.

It is possible, of course, to teach students how to become painters in such a way that they become closed to alternatives and to going beyond the instruction to learn more on their own. This happens when teachers adopt a controlling role and concentrate solely on what students "need" to know. Vocational and technical training should be done with a mind toward opening the students to the exciting possibilities existing in their fields, and to the possibilities of further education or training. Vocational and technical training courses should be taught by teachers using a facilitating role to the fullest extent possible.

This third recommendation relates to flexibility in what is taught in high schools, what is taught in elementary schools that is beyond the compentency level, and how it is taught. For far too long, people have looked down their noses at high school students who are interested in vocational preparation. Instead of recognizing the importance of such preparation, teachers usually advise their "better" students to prepare for college and their "poorer" students to enter vocations. In the meantime, the "poorer" students must study watered-down and meaningless college preparatory courses because this is usually the only alternative. There must be greater flexibility for individualizing goals within courses as well as the objectives of combinations of courses.

Recommendation IV. No student should be permitted to leave the elementary school until competent in the basic areas of communication — the three R's. Schools are remiss if they do not demand that students learn that which is necessary for maintenance of self if it is at all possible for them to learn it. No one can question the need of students to be able to read newspapers, to write legibly and understandably, and to do the arithmetic which is required for everyday living. What is open to question is, "How much does a student need to know?" There is no simple answer to this question, and it should not be settled by opinion. It can be answered by research.

It is possible, though, to define minimum levels of competence. For example, minimum competence in reading might be set for the average student's achievement at the end of grade 6. Or the reading standard could be set in terms of being able to read and understand things such as application forms, automobile drivers' instruction books, drivers' tests, traffic control signs, the daily newspaper (not necessarily the editorial page), etc. Some schools already require competence of this type before high school graduation.

Competence in the area of arithmetic can be defined more easily to include (but not be limited to) the fundamental processes of adding, subtracting, multiplying, and dividing. These processes, in turn, can be defined in terms of the complexity of the problems in which they are to be used. Likewise, arithmetic competence can be defined in terms of the kinds of problems students should be able to solve. For language competence, schools can decide what words people need to know and be able to spell correctly. Writing competence can be defined in terms of use.

There are many difficult problems of measurement involved in such operational definitions of competence. People who desire to develop competency testing programs are urged to consult with test construction specialists. Test construction is not the simple procedure which many people believe it is, and many students are being harmed today by inadequately constructed competency tests. A major problem in the construction of such tests is the question, "What do students need to be minimally competent?" Many school systems which have adopted competency testing have tended to state their criteria in terms of what is *desirable* for students to know, not in terms of what students *need* to know.

Maximum flexibility in curriculum requirements and teaching methodology has been recommended. Students should be taught by facilitating teachers to the limit of their ability to profit from it. At the end of grade 5, children's progress in each of the three R's should be assessed. If deficient in any of these, they should be removed from their regular classrooms for special instruction in the subjects in which they are failing to develop competence. These classes should be scheduled at the same time as instruction in these subjects is given in their regular classrooms. Students in these special classes should be placed in their regular classrooms during the remainder of the school day.

The special classes should not attempt to supplement regular classroom instruction. Instead, they should supplant that instruction. Instructional methodologies would be more restrictive and more controlling. Students would be given less choice in what they could study, how much they could study, and when they could study it. Behavior modification could be used to teach for competency. Appropriate assignments would be made, teachers would monitor students' learning, teachers would guide students and focus them on what they must learn. The students would be reinforced appropriately for their success. Such a plan of instruction, without behavior modification, is developing in many classrooms as a result of periodic achievement testing. This is unfortunate since students are being closed to their experience before they have proved to need this kind of instruction.

There must be provision for the exclusion of some children from mastery or whatever is decided upon as minimum competence. Some children, through no fault of their own, are unable to reach any reasonable standard of competence under any teaching methodology. Schools must know that students have tried and tried long enough before they are exempted from the standard. If minimum competence were set at a level most children could achieve by the end of grade 6 and there are children not showing reasonable progress toward this standard by the end of eight years of schooling, their formal education probably should be terminated. The consequences of continued failure for students and for society must be considered. Schools must be realistic both in what they demand from young people and what young people can produce. If students placed in special classes for competency instruction are not making progress toward this goal, they should be required to continue in school until they are competent if they have the capacity. They should be retained in special classes in elementary schools, though, and not promoted to high school.

Recommendation V. Unless high schools can be modified to be more need-relevant for the many students who enter them and do not continue on to college, compulsory attendance laws must be modified. It is recommended that all children should be compelled to attend school for eight years and until they have passed the minimum competency test. If at the end of eight years they have not passed the competency test, they should not be promoted to high school until they do. The one exception to this is those children who satisfy us that they are unable to learn at this level. If students do not pass the competency test, their formal education should be terminated.

At the point of successful completion of the eighth grade, children should be given a choice of continuing their education either toward vocational and technical goals or toward college-level objectives. There is no advantage to society or other students to compel some students to remain in school beyond the basic competency level if schools do not present them with meaningful options. *The data and conclusions presented in this book show that nonrelevant studies destroy people.*

Students who are forced to remain in school beyond the point of need-relevance require undue amounts of teachers' time to control them. They detract from the opportunities other students have for learning and what seems important to them. Equally bad are the effects on the students who are forced to remain in school in non-need-relevant programs. They become bitter, reject society and its institutions, and often fail to make the contributions which they might have made. We delude ourselves if we think that such young people learn anything of significance under these circumstances. What they learn has negative consequences for all who are involved.

Furthermore, all students do not need a college education. If they are not challenged by college preparatory studies, they should not be destroyed or allowed to disrupt the learnings of other students. Those who remain in school can profit from the resulting smaller classes and greater personal contact with teachers. Compulsory education should not be used as a means of keeping people out of the job market. If they are to be kept out, the schools should not be abused by using them as the agency.

References

APA 84th Annual Convention Program — September 3-September 7, 1976. Washington: American Psychological Association, 1976.

APA Monitor. The Burt affair...Sleuthing in science. Washington: American Psychological Association. 7:12, December, 1976.

Barbakow, D. R. *A Study of Violence in a Southern Metropolitan School System.* The University of Alabama, unpublished doctoral dissertation, 1976.

Bills, R. E. The effect of a value on learning. *Journal of Personality,* 21, 1952, 217-222.

Bills, R. E. Rorschach characteristics of persons scoring high and low in acceptance of self. *Journal of Consulting Psychology,* 1953, 17, 36-38.

Bills, R. E. A comparison of scores on The Index of Adjustment and Values with behavior in level of aspiration tasks. *Journal of Consulting Psychology,* 1953, 17, 206-212.

Bills, R. E. Acceptance of self as measured by interviews and The Index of Adjustment and Values. *Journal of Consulting Psychology,* 1954, 18, p 22.

Bills, R. E. Self concepts and Rorschach signs of depression. *Journal of Consulting Psychology,* 1954, 18, 135-137.

Bills, R. E. *About People and Teaching.* Lexington: University of Kentucky, Bureau of School Service, 1955.

Bills, R. E. Perceptions of self and others of parochial and public school children. *Proceedings: Mid-South Educational Research Association, 3,* November, 1974, p 62.

Bills, R. E. *A System for Assessing Affectivity.* University: The University of Alabama Press, 1975.

Bills, R. E. *Improvement of Instruction through Teacher Description: A Presidential Venture Fund Project.* University: The University of Alabama, 1975.

Bills, R. E. Role concepts of public school teachers. *Proceedings: Mid-South Educational Research Association, 6,* November, 1977, p 75.

Bills, R. E. Summary Data and Interpretations: A System for Assessing Affectivity. *ERIC ED 166 243,* 1978.

Bills, R. E. and Griffin, E. W. Relationships of student sex and race, teacher, sex and race, and teachers' role concepts to student perceptions of teachers' decision-making and interpersonal relationship qualities. *Proceedings: Mid-South Educational Research Association, 8,* November, 1979, 62-63.

Bills, R. E. and McGee, C. R. The effect of attitude toward psychology in a learning experiment. *Journal of Personality, 23,* 1955, 499-500.

Combs, A. W., Richards, A. C. and Richards, F. *Perceptual Psychology.* New York: Harper and Row, 1976.

Emmerling, F. C. *A Study of the Relationships between Personality Characteristics of Classroom Teachers and Pupil Percepts of These Teachers.* Auburn University, Unpublished doctoral dissertation, 1961.

Engle, H. A. *A Study of Openness as a Factor in Change.* Auburn University, unpublished doctoral dissertation, 1961.

Finch, J. D. *Instructor Openness and Student Evaluation of Teaching Effectiveness.* The University of Alabama, unpublished doctoral dissertation, 1973.

Finch, J. D., Finch, C. Bills, and Bills, R. E. Values and school achievement. *Proceedings: Mid-South Educational Research Association, 2,* 1975, 62-63.

Frymier, J. R., Bills, R. E., Russell, J. Frymier, and Finch, C. Bills. A study of oppressive practices in schools. *Curriculum Theory Network,* 4, 1975, 307-313.

Gibran, K. *The Prophet.* New York: Knopf, 1973, p 56.

Green, W. F. A study of racial and socio-economic differences in parental perceptions of their children's schools. *Proceedings: Mid-South Educational Research Association*, 4, 1975, 59.

Henderson, D. C. Improved reading programs at the high school level. *The Counselorgram* (Alabama State Department of Education), 4 (no. 7), 1964, p 1.

Horton, C. S. *Faculty and Student Perceptions of Ideal Teaching Roles in a Small, State University.* The University of Alabama, unpublished doctoral dissertation, 1976.

Houston, C. E. The relationship between classroom decision making processes and feelings about school. The University of Alabama, unpublished paper, 1978.

Kamin, L. J. *The Science and Politics of IQ.* New York: John Wiley and Sons, 1974.

The Miami Herald, 71 (no. 71), February 9, 1981, p 1.

Minder, C. A study of male and female factor structure on the FAS. *Proceedings: Mid-South Educational Research Association*, 4, 1975, 63.

Minder, C. *Teacher Openness As a Function of Race.* The University of Alabama, unpublished doctoral dissertation, 1976.

Nevin, D. and Bills, R. E. *The Schools That Fear Built.* Washington: Acropolis Books Ltd., 1976.

National Institute of Education. *Violent Schools—Safe Schools. The Safe School Study Report to the Congress. Vols. I and II.* February, 1978. *ERIC* ED 149 464 and ED 149 465.

National Institute of Education. *Violent Schools—Safe Schools. The Safe Study Report to the Congress. Executive Summary. ERIC* ED 149 466.

Osgood, C. E. *Method and Theory in Experimental Psychology.* New York: Oxford University Press, 1953.

Phillips, D. J. *Teachers' Role Concepts and the Qualities of Teacher-Student Relationships.* The University of Alabama, unpublished doctoral dissertation, 1978.

Presse, N. J. *Students' Perceptions of the Decision-Making Process and Quality of Relations with Teachers as a Function of Race.* The University of Alabama, unpublished doctoral dissertation, 1977.

Presse, N. J. and Bills, R. E. A comparison of role concepts between public and parochial school teachers. *Proceedings: Mid-South Educational Research Association*, 7, November, 1978, p 118.

Rogers, C. R. *On Becoming a Person.* Boston: Houghton-Mifflin, 1961.

Rogers, C. R. and Skinner, B. F. Some issues concerning the control of human behavior. Unpublished debate, Chicago, 64th Annual Convention of the American Psychological Association, September, 1956.

Shoben, E. J., Jr. The new student: Implications for personnel work. *CAPS, Capsule,* Fall 1968, Vol. 2, No. 1, p 2.

Snygg, D. and Combs, A. W. *Individual Behavior.* New York: Harper, 1949.

Zajonc, R. B. Family configuration and intelligence. *Science,* 192, 4236, April 16, 1976, 227-236.

Index

A

Academies, 32

Academy and Charitable School in the Province of Pennsylvania, 32

Achievement, standards for, 24

Alice in Wonderland, 172

American education and change, 29

Army General Classification Test, 164

Asher, E. J., 164

Association for Supervision and Curriculum Development, 99

Attitudes and learning, 172-173

B

Background for college, 221

Barbakow, D. R., 77, 81, 84, 227

Basic education, 27

Behavior modification, 170

Belief and behavior, 172

Bills, R. E., 72, 84, 97, 110, 122, 142, 183, 227, 229, 230

Binet, A., 160, 161

Bipolar factor, defined, 115

Brown, D. R., 9

Burger, W., 22

Burt, C., 165

C

Carroll, Lewis, 172

Changing behavior in schools, 201

Classroom decision-making, optimal balance, 74
options, 74

College and Academy of Philadelphia, 32

IQ, computation of, 23, 159
  constancy of, 164
  and environment, 164

J

Jensen, A. 165
Junior high schools, 41

K

Kamin, L. J., 161, 165, 168, 230

L

Language learning, and meaning, 190
Latent learning, 177
Latin grammar schools, 29
Latin, study of, 30, 31, 32
Lawhon, B., 42
Learning, and behavior change, 113
  and defensiveness, 202
  and differentiation, 177
  and perceptual variables, 203
Level of regard, defined, 78
Locke, J., 25

M

McGehee, C. R., 172, 183, 229
"Macho" role stereotype, 130
Markus, G. B., 165
Mastery learning, 43
"Me" generation, 54
Meaning, and behavior, 177-179

symbolization of, 196
Mental discipline, 32
Middle schools, 41
  and departmentalization of instruction, 41, 86
Minder, C., 88, 97, 136, 137, 142, 230
Monitoring students' learning, defined, 118-119
Moral values, 22
Motivation, 21
  and teaching, 21
Myths, defined, 17
  and progress, 27

N

National Defense Education Act, 38, 55, 57
National defense and exploitation, 55
National Institute of Education, 58-59, 60, 77, 81, 84, 229
National Science Foundation, 38
  curriculum projects, 56
Negative self-ideal self discrepancy, 66-68
Nevin, D., 64, 72, 122, 123, 230
Normal distribution, 22
"Now" generation, 54
Northwest Ordinance, 154

O

"Old Deluder Satan Act," 30-31
Open schools, 42-46
Opening or focussing, defined, 116-117

Openness, defined, 132
  and evaluation, 194
  to experience, 78, 193-194
  and physiological factors, 207
  and threat, 195
Operant conditioning, 148
Oppression, defined, 110
  source of, 105
Oppressive practices, categories of, 102-103
  and depersonalization, 106
  frequency of, 103
  and race, 107
  and rules, 105
  and school codes, 105
  and sex, 107
  and student rebellion, 104
Osgood, C. E., 174, 183, 230

P

Parents' goals for schools, 93
People as passive reactors, 186
Perception, and behavior, 201
  and diet, 176
  and experience, 175-176
  and need, 174
  and physiology, 175
  and value, 175
  and toxic or chemical poisons, 175
Perceptual change, and meaning, 205
Perceptual consistency, 171, 173
Perceptual constancy, 173
  and personality, 187, 192
Perceptual field, kaleidoscopic nature of, 192
  stability of, 192
  structure of, 198

Perceptual theory, first assumption, 185
  second assumption, 186
Personality, adequacy of 206
  defined, 187
Phenomenal field, and behavior, 172
  and reality, 180
Phillips Academy of Andover, 32
Phillips, D. J., 142, 230
Planning with or planning for, defined, 117-118
Positive self-ideal self discrepancy, 66-68
Presse, N. J., Jr., 121, 123, 142, 230
Psychological illness, and non-relevance of school learning, 225
  and threat, 197
Psychology and child rearing, 52
Public Latin School of Boston, 29

R

Reinforcement, defined, 150
  and bribes, 170
Responsibility, factors in, 146
Responsibility for learning, defined, 119-120
Retroactive inhibition, 202
Richards, A. C., 180, 183, 200, 210, 229
Richards, F., 180, 183, 200, 210, 229
Rogers, C. R., 9, 10, 113, 122, 131, 132, 147, 152, 153, 156, 168, 194, 200, 230, 231
Role concepts, departmentalized teachers, 205

T

Tax supported schools, 30

Teacher behavior, and students' attitudes, 88

Teacher openness, measurement of, 132

Teacher problems, dimensions of, 133

Teacher roles, and school organization, 212
and school oppression, 212

Teacher-student planning, 209

Teaching, defined, 112
goals of, 112

Teaching effectiveness, and block-of-time teaching, 218
and class size, 212
and departmentalization, 212
and psychological distance, 211
and school size, 221
and self-contained classrooms, 218
and student differences, 217

Teaching goals, and 50-minute periods, 214

Teachers' role concepts, elementary, 129
secondary, 129

Teaching roles, factors in, 116

Teaching and communication, 25

Teaching makes students alike, 24

Terman, L., 161

Thorndike, E. L., 32

Threat, and abnormal psychology, 196
and change, 198-199, 206
and defensiveness, 198

defined, 195
and development of intelligence, 197
and evaluation, 198
and helping relationships, 198
and locus of responsibility, 198
and meaning, 197
and schooling, 207
source of, 196-197
and teachers' problems, 197-198

Through the Looking Glass, 172

Traditional schools, 44

Tutorial teaching, 210

U

Unconditionality of regard, defined, 78

U.S. Department of Interior, 20

V

Validity of educational practices, 18

Vandalism and violence, 58, 77, 81

Y

Yerkes, R., 161

Z

Zajonc, R. B., 168, 231